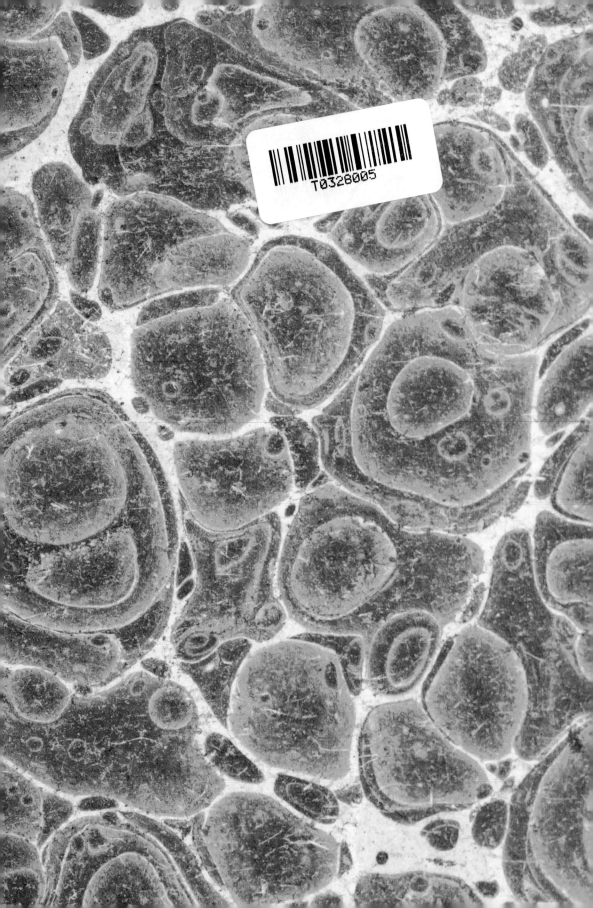

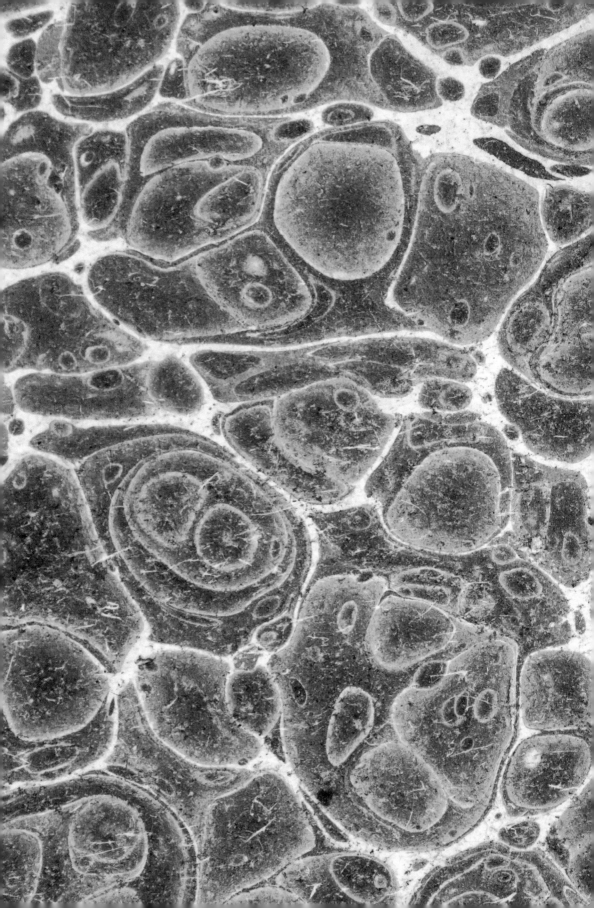

TWINKIND

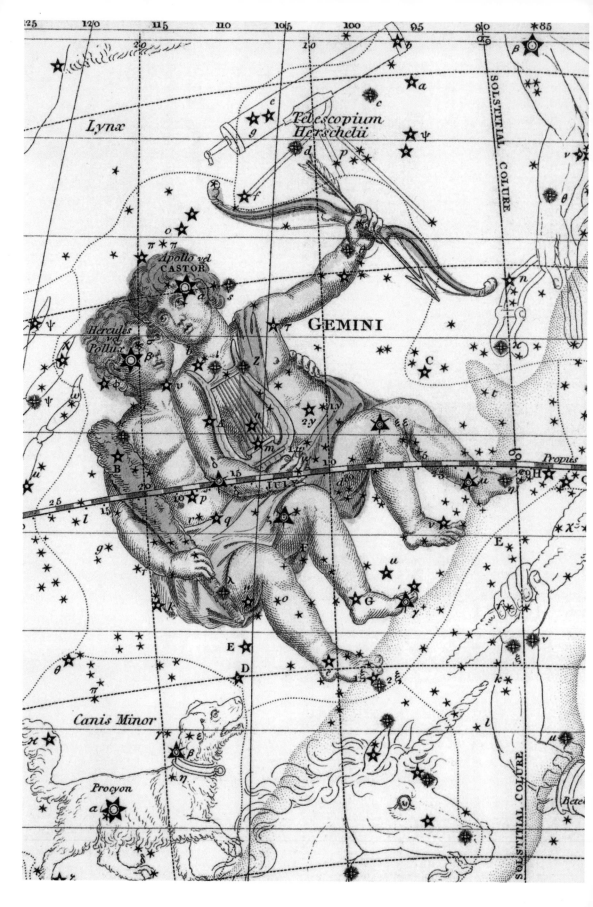

TWINKIND

THE SINGULAR SIGNIFICANCE OF TWINS

WILLIAM VINEY
Foreword **GEORGE VINEY**

THE BYRTHE FYGVRES

CONTENTS

✳ ✳

Will was born first, by about 12 minutes. Nearly all siblings experience rivalry, and with so few physical differences to separate them, it can be especially intense between identical twins. You can therefore appreciate my satisfaction at having the opportunity to write this foreword, and get a word in edgeways.

'What's it like to be a twin?' has been a top-three question to ask us about our relationship. The lazy answer was always to shrug and say, 'I don't know. I don't know what it's like not to be a twin'. The longer, less evasive and more complicated answer touches on a set of contradictions – involving rarity and plurality, visibility and mistaken identity, community and isolation. It also depends on age and circumstances.

'Did you play tricks on your teachers at school?' was another question, accompanied by a hopeful look. We enjoyed giving people disappointment. Teachers would trick themselves without any effort on our part or retreat to the safety of 'Mr Viney'. Whilst impersonating one another was too easy to be much fun, there was a hidden truth to our reluctance. We protected our own paths, something actively encouraged by our parents. As small children, matching outfits were an occasional novelty rather than the norm.

As we grow older and less insecure, it is amusing to observe our tastes and habits

GEORGE (LEFT) AND WILLIAM VINEY
Photographer Camilla Jessel lived close to the twins' maternal grandfather and this picture appeared in her book, *Where is Baby?* (1986). The overalls, colour-coded blue and green to tell the twins apart, were made by their mother.

converge. We chose to live together in our 20s and got along well instead of merely tolerating each other's presence, as we did in our adolescence. Now, both married with children, we celebrate our birthdays together with an annual Big Lunch. We enjoy ordering the same things to eat and often give one another clothes, confident that our own choice of style and fit will please the other. Is this nature, nurture, or a pleasurable and uncertain combination of the two?

An interest in twins appears to be universal. Twins are common enough to be familiar to all, but scarce enough to remain a curiosity. This wonderful book demonstrates in lush detail that twins have forever fascinated humankind. Its chapters reveal the abundance and variety of responses that twins have inspired – from veneration to violence and everything in between. The duality of twins is a gift to creativity of all sorts, inspiring myth and romance, farce and horror, spiritualism and the sciences. From this cultural debris the character and ideas of the twins themselves are occasionally perceived. More often, twins' visual memorabilia both projects and reflects the preoccupations of the singleton societies into which twins are born.

We grew up playing lots of sports, encouraged by our father, who enjoyed imagining us as professional footballers. Assuming the tone and excitement of an eager sportscaster, he would comment on our games in the garden: 'Viney passes to Viney, who plays a one-two with Viney, and ... Viney scores!' Naturally, we each wanted to be the goal scorer. In this instance, I am delighted to make no mistake by passing him the ball.

Fantastic, enchanting, eerie and strange – welcome to a multiple metropolis: a twin town for all who fear and revere people born as two. Since records began, twin people have been dug from the earth, plucked from the skies, honoured as gods, anointed as kings and queens, and made host to every possible being. Their contemporary importance is built on ancient myth and legend, but twins are also figures of promise and futurity. They are symbols used to guide modern lives, formed into tools that aid different kinds of technical discoveries. Meanwhile, their existence, variety, and meaning around the world challenges folk wisdom and scientific expertise in equal measure.

Every twin is part of a duo, each twin pair is a member of a group of twins, and every group of twins is known differently to their non-twin audiences. No two twins are exactly alike. Nor can each pair fully represent another as a substitute or supernumerary. They, too, are singular. And yet there is a stubborn and persistent relationship between twins: sameness, enduring intimacy and expected cooperation. This book shows how twins fulfil and defy these and other expectations. The cultural life of twins continues to evolve, shapeshift and break rank, synchronize and switch places with the single-born.

For me, writing about twins means reconciling my own limited experience

PORTRAIT OF SWADDLED TWINS
In *The Early-Deceased Children of Jacob de Graeff and Aeltge Boelens* (c. 1617) the face of one twin is darker than the other. It suggests they suffered from twin-to-twin transfusion syndrome – a shared placenta supplied too much blood to one and too little to the other.

of being a twin with the vast diversity of twin experience in written and visual records. This connects to how being a twin is a baffling and powerful combination of effort and ease. We do nothing to choose being twins at birth; we are born and form with time. But we become part of a group of people constructed from an elaborate thread of different cultural practices – woven and unwoven, threaded and frayed according to time, place and perspective. And so being a twin involves not one person or two, but a multitude of different people.

Every past, present and future is accompanied by twin visions, each expressing different ways to understand an element of human nature or potential. Twins have been used to measure standards and to project old and new norms for what humans are capable of doing. Untethered from the acceptable or standard notions that guide the lives of the majority, twins are available to guide diverse mythological, religious, experimental, artistic and commercial ideas. This is the history we live and live differently to those born alone.

Transfigured as gods and monsters, spirits and animal familiars, and viewed as phantoms, freaks and clones, twins pass through a hall of unpredictable mirrors. These are contorted according to changing ideas about what defines twin people, what makes them different from or alike to each other, and what separates them from non-twins. Each figure reveals the changing assumptions and desires that the single-born majority have for twins and for themselves.

Twins attract enormous curiosity. They are said to be unique among humans for . possessing an unusual intimacy, understanding, sympathy and empathy for the other. When

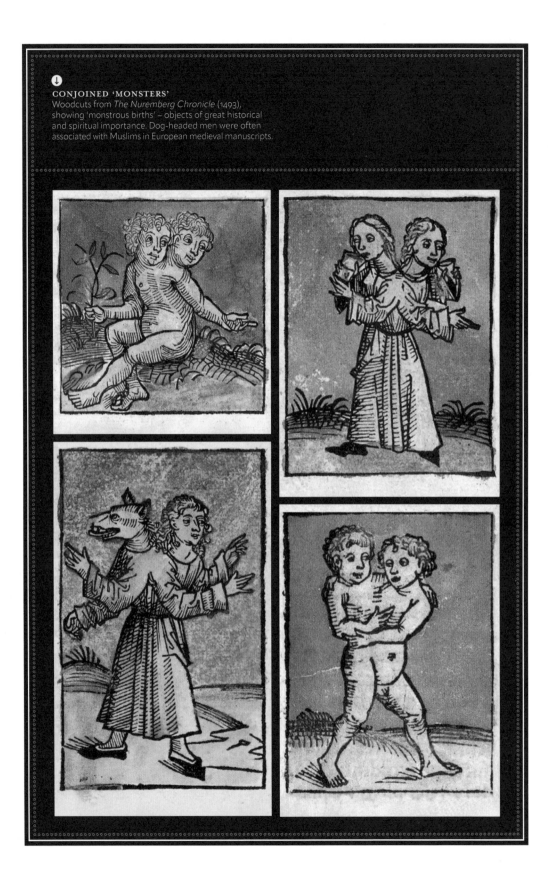

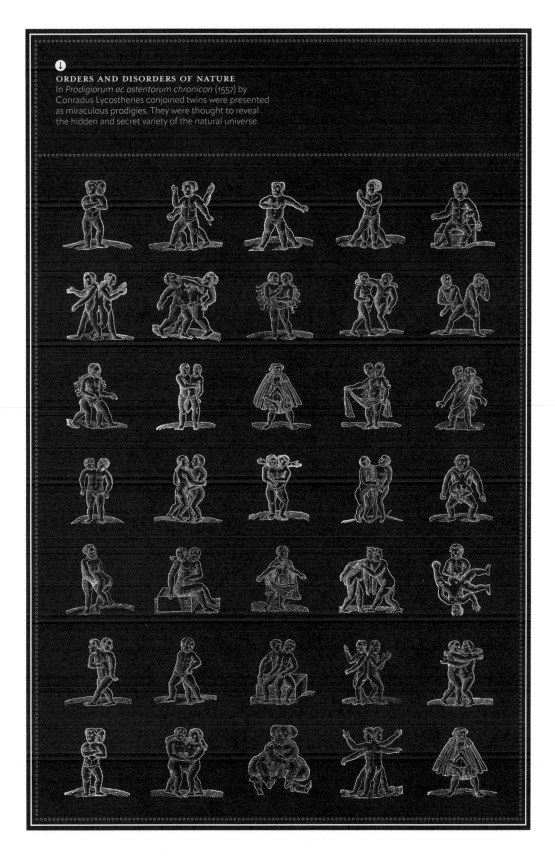

↓

ORDERS AND DISORDERS OF NATURE
In *Prodigiorum ac ostentorum chronicon* (1557) by
Conradus Lycosthenes conjoined twins were presented
as miraculous prodigies. They were thought to reveal
the hidden and secret variety of the natural universe.

**CORNELIA AND
JAMES WILSON**
The twelve-year-old Wilson
twins were photographed by
documentary photographer
Lewis Hine in 1912. They were
the third set of twins to be
born to their parents.

**DANIEL AND
ANGELO PENTO**
The Pento twins, with their
older brother John, were
seven years old and selling
newspapers in Hartford,
Connecticut, when they
were photographed in 1909.

twins account for themselves, they do so
on prefabricated terms: What kind of twin
are you? Are you similar? How close? How
telepathic? Are you sure? I find such questions
demand a certain kind of performance art and
a raw choice between evasion or disclosure.
I give my view. But I give it in relation to
my changing thoughts and feelings about
twinning, and to a widening understanding
of twins in the world.

It takes a lifetime to accept what you are
to other people. But as twins we are a thing to
look at and scrutinize. In our middle age, my
brother and I remain aware of the spontaneous
smile of recognition on the face of a passer-by.
Some people are compelled to stare. When
we were children, our mother dressed us in
different colours to avoid confusion. She had
a camera ready for every jam-smothered grin
of our childhood years. These photographs are
small, unique and personal.

In the 1980s, one image of us appeared in
a book for younger children, printed on thick,
gnawable board. We are both sockless, our
feet splayed like happy seals, and dressed in
pastel-striped dungarees. We are perched on
a chair whose back acts as a cover for him and
a parapet for me. He looks through wooden
slats with a broad and knowing grin, while my
inter-lunar stare focuses on a point beyond
the camera's lens. It took time for us to
know why our image gave young children
something to get their teeth into.

This image resonates with countless other
pictures of twins – stilled in time, lined up
next to each other, placed in a visual parallel
that creates a comparative dialogue. We are
pillars of whatever difference or similarity
or remarkable quirk you may want to see.

When looking at images of twins such
as these, we may believe that the spectacle
is of interest only to the viewer. But twins
are always learning about what your curiosity
looks like. There are millions of twin images,
and together they reflect collective interests
rather more than they document the varieties
of twin life and experience. Perhaps this is
why they tend to follow certain patterns,
poses and gestures that make twins even more
recognizable – a set of tricks that make some
twin people more twin than others. This visual
economy ensures some images circulate while
others lose their momentum.

For a long time, I was spared the ambition
of writing about twins. But in 2012 the vocation
caught up with me. There was no great
epiphany but a realization that twins were
waiting for me in libraries, laboratories and
conferences, and at other events, often in
the company of experts who pursued twins
with professional zeal – scientists, clinicians,
psychologists, parents and other carers, artists,
writers, filmmakers and other technologists.
I became profoundly interested in the
experience of being a twin, and the knowledge
inspired by twins and twin data. I realized
that my own life was very much tangled up in
this history, and I wanted to make sense of it.

Until this point, I had found that the
problem of being a twin was that everyone
else seemed to get far more out of it than me.
I could not understand the sense of excitement
people got from twins. It was mundane and
disenchanting to me – rarely an advantage and
often a source of frustration. Things started
to change as I realized I could explore the
curiosity of others. It took time to undo and
even unlearn much of what I thought was

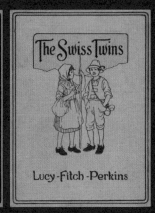

TWINS FEATURED IN CHILDREN'S BOOKS
Repetition and familiarity are staples of children's books. In these three series, published from 1904 to 1934, each pair of twins is easily drawn into comic mishap or misadventure.

THOSE TIRESOME TWINS, 1905
The twins in Blanche Handler's picture book are physically alike, highly collaborative and charmingly mischievous. Their activities are narrated in rhyming couplets.

consensus or undisputed fact. Writing this book helped. I would not call it healing or therapy. Perhaps it has been a slow letting loose, an unwinding of individual and collective stories.

When you grow up in rural England in the 1980s and 1990s, everyone knows who you are. Unless you are twins. Then you are an indistinguishable oddity, a known unknown. Anonymity can be a pleasure, unless it is forced on you. Yet even our anonymity was shared and, therefore, incomplete. After time apart, living in different cities and out of touch, my brother and I moved into a London flat together. We spent our Sunday evenings during the financial crisis of 2007–08 discussing the likelihood of him losing his job buying and selling shares. At that time I had a different kind of uncertain future, working part-time in publishing and studying for another degree. Having lost our relation to the near future we were free to contemplate whether our present was any more or less anonymous as before. Although we occupied the same household, it was not clear if we were growing together or growing apart. But our lives were already packaged into stories based on our relation to one another to be told in two parts.

Reflecting on lives lived and lives foregone, British novelist Hilary Mantel (1952–2022) once imagined being haunted by a series of ghostly choices that halo each decision, preference or accident:

When you turn and look back down the years, you glimpse the ghosts of other lives you might have led; all houses are haunted. The wraiths and phantoms creep under your carpets and between the warp and weft of fabric, they lurk in wardrobes and lie flat under drawer-liners. You think of the children you might have had but didn't. When the midwife says, 'It's a boy,' where does the girl go?[1]

The 'haunting' Mantel describes is also ghosted by biography's individualism, its writerly dedication to putting one sentence before the next, and the serial belief that each event erases the possibility of another. Being tracked by the memories of other lives also accompanies twin siblings. For twins, these alternatives are partially manifested in another person's life choices – the glimpsing and creeping and lurking are not simply imagined. For Mantel, a sense of the present can be understood through these visions of the past, irrevocably foregone. But from where and from what historical 'when' does this style of thinking begin or end for twins?

'Vanishing twin syndrome' is the name given to the miscarriage of one foetus and the survival of another. It is said to affect as many as 36 per cent of twin pregnancies.[2] There is no way to generalize about the loss of a twin at any stage of the life course. The possibility or loss of a twin serves as a reminder – how we tell stories about ourselves can challenge us to consider the units we use to narrate life together. In this twins are unusual for how they experience their place in the world in relation to others. Until and including the last act, each twin is another's negative portrait that may embody life's forsaken paths, even as each enters the gothic house alone.

Pictures of twins appear to us via the aesthetic choices and conventions of painters, photographers, writers and other artists – or

We're Twins, as everyone can see,
And nobody knows her from me.

We are so glad that we are two,
If we were one, what should we do?

They never seem to think,—it's strange
How easy it will be to change.

Since being ill is bad enough,

The Other takes the doctor's stuff.

Beside the door there is a place,
Where we are put when in disgrace.

We met Aunt Emma in the street,
She says it's very wrong to cheat.

And we shall never, that is plain,
Know which of us is which again.

When we go up to bed at night
Sometimes we have a pillow-fight.

➡ / ⊘
ZWILLINGE, 1977
Photographs of Richard
Kriesche's (b. 1940)
performance artwork.
Each twin 'performs' next
to surveillance footage of
their sibling, who is sitting
in the room next door.

according to the number-crunching analysis of data-driven reason. The angle of a camera, the touch of a painter's brush or the white blood cells numbered in a sample – are just some of the many ways that twin data are placed into sequence, series and rank. During our time living together in London, we visited a laboratory, where our blood was drawn from our veins and our organs were made to perform. Split up into more parts, we gave up our saliva, urine and other samples, uncertain about what would happen to the genetic and other molecular data sequenced from them. Our embarrassed bodies were scanned using advanced techniques that stripped away the flesh and tissue that made us look so alike, leaving only our skeletons outlined. We were reassembled on screens. These samples and images, all our measurements, were entered into data systems with those of thousands of other twins. They were banked for scientific research in one of the most detailed cohorts of twin data anywhere in the world. The future uses of our health data are likely to follow scientific interests, fashion and finance.

We were eligible for this voluntary and intense process of data extraction because we were adult twins: there were no other criteria. I would later learn that the scientific use of twins was a relatively modern invention, created in northern Europe towards the end of the 19th century and industrialized as a set of research methods at the beginning of the 20th century. Although we qualified to be part of these scientific experiments because of how we were born, there was so much that was changing and contingent about our participation in biomedical research. This attention was quite different to the attention

I had known before, the methods and motivations for comparison unfamiliar to me. Anonymized again and made into numbers, we were valued as subjects, aligned to biological types. It was fascinating to learn how twins held different value for different communities, whose significance, in turn, depended on different methods of comparison. Being in a science laboratory made me appreciate that looking at twins is something all cultures do. They enlarge the influence of twins, as a people that make certain kinds of knowledge possible.

US journalist Lawrence Wright (b. 1947) says that 'twins pose questions we might not think to ask if we lived without them ... their mere existence allows us to test certain ideas about how we are the way we are'.[3] I think the thought experiment is meant to capture the subtle but profound importance of twins to the formation of human culture. But I would not have very many ideas if twins did not exist. And I wonder what more would be learnt if we asked how twins actually pose those profound questions – under what historical conditions, with what media and methods of magic, art and science?

This book has been designed as a navigation tool for these and other questions. It also serves as a visual portal to a community of people often known in stereo, whose views and opinions about being twins are rarely heard. Like other augmented realities, the imagined places and psychological realms occupied by twins make utopian and dystopian worlds possible. Those of us who are born as twins must live and negotiate these competing visions of twin life. It is all I have ever known, but the culture I live in is still changing the rules of the game. Some of us are more or

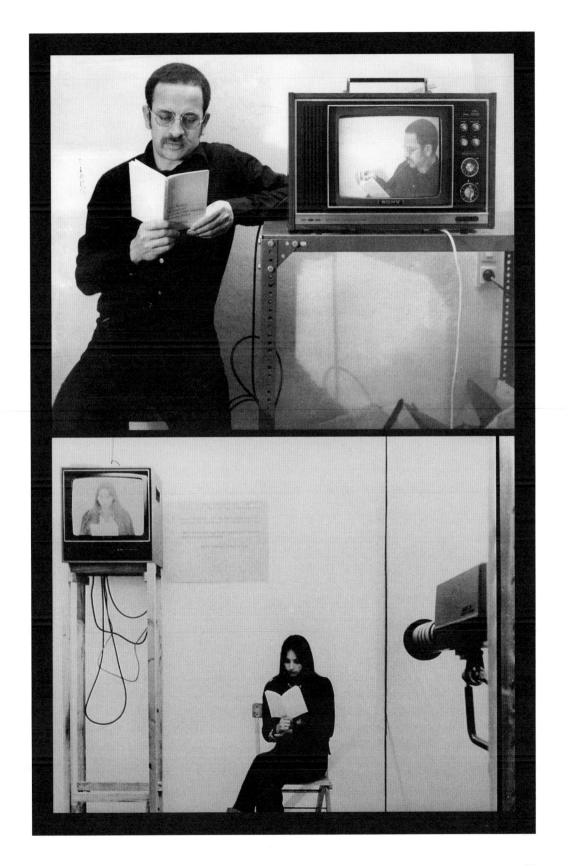

MARCOS AND MAURCIOUS
Part of the *Duo Morality* series (2010) by Noga Shtainer (b. 1982), these identical twins were photographed in Cândido Gódoi, Brazil, a village with an inexplicably high twin birth rate.

TWINS DAY FESTIVAL
Twins pose for photographs on 29 May 2017 during the 11th Twins Rafting Festival. One hundred and thirty sets of twins gathered at the event at Yuxi Grand Canyon, Henan Province, China.

less satisfied with what is on offer. Few can follow every twin convention or none.

Twin birth rates vary according to geography, age, ethnicity, reproductive behaviour, diet and access to advanced medical technologies that include capacities to induce and preserve twin conceptions. Being a twin concerns many other people: not only family members, parents and siblings, but scientists, medical and other health professionals. Unsurprisingly, there have never been more twins walking the planet. About 1.6 million twin pairs are born each year. On average, white European and North American populations currently have 19 twin births per 1,000 deliveries. In Southeast Asia, this figure is 6 to 9 twin births, and in South America about 9 in every 1,000 live births are twins. Western and Central African populations have the highest twin birth rates, at 18 per 1,000 live births, without accessing advanced fertility treatments.[4]

Across history, twins have been continuously cut apart from singletons. While twins are a numerical minority compared to people born alone, they are not always minor players in social or historical terms. Twins can generate the deepest attraction and respect, but also serve as the pinnacle of disgust and horror. Twins are cultural riddles. But at this level, they remain individually powerless to decide how they are valued, divided from what others take them to be. The causes and consequences of separating twins may bring glory or it may bring irreparable harm.

In recent decades campaigners for racial, gender, sexual and disability justice have shown that knowledge depends on relations to power, and these insights are the common ground for solidarity. Lived experience has grounded different social movements and their demands for change, based on what specific communities endure and survive. Slogans emerging from these different movements have often linked community experience with collective demands for political inclusion, justice and freedom from violence (e.g. 'Nothing about us without us', #MeToo, #BlackLivesMatter). The personal is also political for twin people, but in ways that have not formed part of a social movement. Their lived experience can be a source of evidence – the texture of a shared reality that frequently contrasts with the cultural values imposed upon them.

There exists a more abstract history to hold against the important experience of twins living in the 21st century. It resides in the great foundation narratives of ancient societies, epic stories, cosmic legends and astrological tales used as the basis of current and obsolete religious and philosophical belief systems. This book follows some of these stories and the visual language they utilize. It is not a perfect or perfectly inclusive history (if such a thing were possible). But it shows the way towards a history that is dynamic, discrete and collective. And it asks if twins can imagine alternatives to the collectives into which they are born. ✳✳

PART ONE

✿ ✿

MYTH + LEGEND

MYTH + LEGEND

✿ ✿

⚝ ⚝

At the dawn of recorded time, so twins appear, illuminating the origins of the world and the values of human beings. It is a role of both power and service. In many creation stories twins are deities, as they are seen as makers of life and the cosmos. They are said to form light and dark, day and night, sun and moon, earth and wind and fire. Each person lives as a consequence of these twin creators, leaders and heroes. And since many religions picture a creator god or supreme being at the start of a human world, twins are found in their company as intermediaries between divine and human affairs.

Ancient Egyptians celebrated hundreds of gods and gave them roles that changed over dynasties, and between cities.[1] Core to the Heliopolitan group is the creator god Atum, whose subsequent generations or 'developments' include the deities Shu and Tefnut, Geb and Nut, Osiris, Isis, Seth and Nephthys. This creation myth, prominent during the Old Kingdom era approximately 2500 BC, begins with Atum – associated with the sun god Re – dwelling upon and then dividing primeval, undifferentiated waters. As an androgynous creator god depicted in human form, Atum is said to orgasm and spit his semen (some sources say sneeze) to make two counterpart beings. The source for all differentiation, and the possibility for all further development, manifests in these twins, Shu and Tefnut – the first male and female deities. Atum, fully realized, is without division; his name means 'he who makes complete' and 'finisher'. His autoerotic twin creations are the foundations of every life that follows: air (Shu) and moisture (Tefnut). It is via twins that a primordial atmosphere forms a new cosmos that accommodates humans.

According to this tradition, Atum's next developments are Shu and Tefnut's children, Nut and Geb, twins closely entangled. Shu is frequently shown astride them, separating Nut, the goddess of the sky, from Geb, her twin brother. Geb and Nut produce Osiris, Isis, Seth and Nephthys. From a primordial creator god comes twins that are separated twice over. The ancient Egyptian cosmos is formed first from asexual reproduction and then a foundation of gendered, mixed-sex twin pairs. They are the first deities – not because they are alike but to create difference amid sameness.

Ancient artefacts relate stories about twins that divide one or none into many. They are mythology's great catalysts. Everywhere, twins kick-start storylines. In Greek traditions, the god of gods is Zeus, who is portrayed as a prolific maker of heroic twins. Zeus's twin offspring are a motif, signs of his fertility and strength. By seduction or force, Zeus has many and various sets of twins. These twins transform who has power and what kinds of beings have godly status in the human world.

Twins are often a product of transgressive contacts between gods and humans. Heracles and Iphicles are one pair conceived when

TWINS BORN OF FIRE
In the Hindu epic *Mahābhārata* a *yajna*, or fire sacrifice ritual, is performed and a young woman and a youth, Draupadi and Dhrishtadyumna, emerge from the fire.

NEFERTITI AND ISIS
Watercolour copy of a wall painting in the tomb of Queen Nefertiti (*c.* 1279–13 BC). Isis, goddess of healing and magic, leads Nefertiti, her twin.

LEDA AND THE SWAN
Infidelity and bestiality create Castor and Pollux,
depicted here alongside their mother, Leda. This
painting is a copy from the 1500s, after the original,
painted by Leonardo da Vinci (1452–1519), was lost.

HERACLES KILLS THE SNAKES
Pompeo Batoni's (1708–87) *The Infant Hercules
Strangling Serpents in his Cradle* (1743) depicts Heracles'
first show of strength. By killing the snakes Heracles
saves his own life and the life of his mortal twin, Iphicles.

Alcmene, the wife of Amphitryon, has sex with both her husband and the god Zeus. The ambiguous family is the creative outcome that structures an epic drama. In this case, the twins do not share fathers. Heracles is the godly son of Zeus and Iphicles the son of Amphitryon. In this and other respects, twin identities belong to comparative, separate and divided worlds, owing extremes to a masculine separation of godly charisma and human ordinariness. But Zeus's wife Hera wants revenge on her cheating husband and tries to kill the twins with venomous snakes. These prove no match for the newborn Heracles, who fights them off with his bare hands. This is the first fearless demonstration of the courage and strength that have come to define Heracles' well-known Labours. As he wrestles the snakes, his mortal twin Iphicles flees. Although newborn twins rarely fight snakes to the death, they might be scrutinized, compared and judged according to qualities that exist both inside and outside their story. Heracles and Iphicles are compared, their stations made; the pairing creates that order and a pattern observed in many other twin myths.

Greek gods bring twins into the lives of humans. Zeus takes the shape of a swan to rape Leda. She then has sex with her husband. Her twins – Castor and Pollux – hatch from eggs and have different fathers, invoking a process now called 'heteropaternal superfecundation'. This reproductive phenomenon is common in some animals but rare among humans. Pollux is a god and Castor a mortal. They are often represented together and known collectively as the Dioscuri (sons of Zeus). They make their adventures as horse-riding heroes, Argonauts and hunters of the Calydonian boar – until Castor is mortally wounded during their final expedition. Pollux bargains with Zeus to prevent being separated from his twin. They agree to share Pollux's immortality with Castor, so the twins spend their days in Hades and their nights in the heavenly constellations. They lend their names to twin stars as figures in the constellation Gemini.

Across cultures, twins have also participated in a greater storytelling series of galloping twin adventurers. As figures that often divide – splitting apart people and communities – they are frequently more than the sum of their parts. Like the Dioscuri, the Ashvins are heroic, horse-riding twins – venerated as heroes of ancient Indic poetry, philosophy and religion. They appear in the *Rigveda* (c. 1500–1000 BC), one of the great Hindu Vedic texts, with their siblings Yama and Yami, further twinned deities in a pantheon full of twins.[2] The Ashvins are also elevated as heroes and 'sons of the sky', made from bestial and adulterous beginnings. Their father, the sun god Surya, is said in some accounts to have conceived the twins by disguising himself as a horse.

The mythological song may be different, but there are recurrent motifs that have encouraged modern historians and archaeologists of ancient societies to conclude that horse-riding hero twins are consistent figures in Proto-Indo-European cultures. Versions of the heavenly twins reappear in Baltic traditions, as the Lithuanian Diẽvo sunẽliai or Latvian Dieva dēli. In the Hindu epic *Mahābhārata* (c. 400 BC–c. AD 200), they

---

✧ ✧

---

① NUT AND GEB
Egyptian gods of the sky and earth depicted, right, in *The Book of the Dead of Henuttawy* (c. 1069–525 BC).

② ISIS AND OSIRIS
Tabakenkhonsu, led by the god Thoth, is presented to Isis and Osiris on this Egyptian funerary stela (c. 680–670 BC).

③ NEPHTHYS AND ISIS
Nephthys is frequently depicted as a mirror to her twin sister, Isis. On this amulet they flank Horus (c. 664–525 BC).

⑤ CASTOR AND POLLUX
The Dioscuri twins – gods who were thought to help shipwrecked sailors – are depicted saving their sister, Helen, from her kidnapper Theseus in this 1817 oil painting by Jean-Bruno Gassies (1786–1832).

④ APOLLO AND ARTEMIS
The divine archers depicted on a Greek volute krater, or mixing vessel (c. 430–400 BC).

⑤ SASSANIAN TWINS
The twins astride their winged horses, depicted on a gilded plate (c. AD 500–600).

recur as Nakula and Sahadeva, adopted sons of the Ashvins, skilled in medicine and horses.[3] Another Hindu epic, *Rāmāyaṇa* (*c.* 300 BC), features twins Lava and Kusha, first children of Rama and Sita. They are born after Sita escapes accusations of adultery and gives birth to twins, who are raised in an ashram and instructed by Valmiki, the alleged author of *Rāmāyaṇa*. The twins later demonstrate their virtues before their estranged father, thereby gaining his recognition. And like Greek and later Roman heroes, Lava and Kusha are said to have founded important cities (modern-day Lahore and Titilagarh).

Oral storytelling traditions can be lost in transcription. How human twins were treated, what they felt, how they viewed their place in ancient societies – this we must glean via the interests of the elite and literate communities doing the storytelling. Archaeological records display just a fraction of the variations. In more recent centuries of conflict and conquest, Western European twin myths account for the greater share of fragments that can be pieced together and discussed by modern scholars. This situation is neither new nor specific to our times.

If archaeological records reflect ancient and more recent historical conflict, some of the earliest Greek sources make Apollo and Artemis brother and sister who are born on different islands. By the 5th century BC, the poet Pindar describes Apollo and Artemis as 'twins and peers of the gods', and their twin relationship develops with time. By the 1st and 2nd centuries BC, their twin nativity is heroically entwined with their mother, Leto, who is chased by Hera to the island of Delos, 'where she gave birth first to Artemis, and

then, with the aid of Artemis as a midwife, to Apollo'.[4] Having helped her mother give birth to her own twin brother, Artemis (or Diana in Roman antiquity) became venerated as a midwife and intercessor in other difficult births.

Historians wonder at the political value of twins in these stories. If the contrast between earlier and later sources of the myth suggests that Apollo and Artemis have been *made* into twins, then what does that tell us about twin births in ancient Greek society? One explanation is that over generations a twin birth has been viewed as a suitably godly birth for two popular deities. Another explanation points to a more political motive – the version of the twins born together on Delos dates to the early 5th century BC, a time when Athens controlled Delos.[5] In this case the birth of mythological twins is a political and historical artefact, one that depends on conflict, economic and religious exchange.

Although reading myths via political optics may involve some guesswork, Judaic and Greco-Roman foundation stories also use twin births to clarify positions of power. The nations of Israel and Edom are born with twins Jacob and Esau, sons of Isaac and Rebecca. They are destined to be antagonists. God said to Rebecca: 'Two nations are in your womb, and two people from within you will be separated; one people will be stronger than the other, and the older will serve the younger' (Gen 25: 23). In myths and religions, twins are not universally heroic figures. They are used opportunistically, forming displays of power and bringing unity and strength to militant cultures and societies.

The city of Rome was also founded by outsider twins: Romulus and Remus, who are

APOLLO AND DIANA
Olympian gods Apollo
and Artemis were known
as Apollo and Diana in the
Roman pantheon. The twins
are depicted here in a 1526
painting by Lucas Cranach
the Elder (c. 1472–1553).

✧✧ ... far-shooting Apollo and
Artemis shooter of arrows,
... desirable children above
all the offspring of Heaven. ✧✧

Hesiod, 'Theogony', c. 730–700 BC

said to be twin brothers. Abandoned as babies by the River Tiber, they are miraculously found and nursed by a she-wolf to become courageous warrior kings. They argue, and Romulus kills Remus. Romulus then founds his namesake city, Rome. This story, a tablet polished over thousands of years of retelling, has not always been presented in this way. Scholars identify earlier legends recounting just one king, Romulus. Remus, they say, is little more than an invention, the outcome of a political agreement between local communities in the 4th century BC. This political settlement required the old myths to be combined and renewed. And so Romulus gained a brother, Remus. Others seek less literal interpretations, pointing to the double meaning of the Latin word for wolf, *lupa* – common slang for 'prostitute' – to emphasize the parts of the story that appealed to a Roman sense of humour.[6] Although it has the enduring elements of a foundation story – disinheritance, abandonment, miraculous salvation, justice and betrayal – the city of Rome is also created and remade.

Tall tales serve as propaganda and popular entertainment. Medieval merchants and aristocrats who wanted to connect papal Rome with other city-states reimagined Remus's fate: he left his brother to found Rome while he travelled north to Siena, where the symbol of the twins can still be found throughout the old city.[7] Condensed and aggregated together, Romulus and Remus are made and undone as twins – founder brothers, murderers, unique and paired.

The foundation stories of Romulus, Remus and the creation of Rome make sibling murder (fratricide) a key part of the city's identity.

Unsurprisingly, the legend was not always popular, particularly with later Christian church leaders such as Augustine (AD 354–430), who wanted a 'city of God' rather than a city founded by twins, raised by wild animals and soaked in brothers' blood. The murder of a twin by their brother was viewed as the city's original sin, resurrected from a pagan era. The religious and political uses of the legend continued to change right into the 20th century. With the rise of Mussolini and Italian fascism in the 1920s, blood sacrifice and fratricide became potent symbols for a militarized state.

The nature of what is recorded about twin myths and their meaning depends on complex geopolitical histories. These histories remain the constant context for twin stories up to the present day. The *Diné Bahane* is the creation myth of the Navajo people of North America. It has been passed down the generations through oral storytelling traditions, and its teachings are a key element in *Diné* history and culture. The first human, Asdzą́ą́ Nádleehé (Changing Woman), gives birth to hero twins – Tóbájíschíní (Born for Water) and Nayee' Neizghání (Monster Slayer) – whose adventures rid the world of monsters. Their actions display the main virtues of Navajo life and their significance is key to protection and healing ceremonials.[8]

Current knowledge of Mesoamerican myths about twins – associated with the Olmec, Zapotec, Maya, Toltec and Aztec peoples – is shaped by European colonization and the widespread destruction of indigenous texts and other artefacts. Material remains such as the ancient *Popol Vuh* panels survive to explain the importance the Maya people

ROMULUS AND REMUS MOSAIC
This mosaic (*c.* AD 300–400) was found in North Yorkshire, England, during excavations in the 1840s. It depicts twins Romulus and Remus with the she-wolf who, according to legend, raised them.

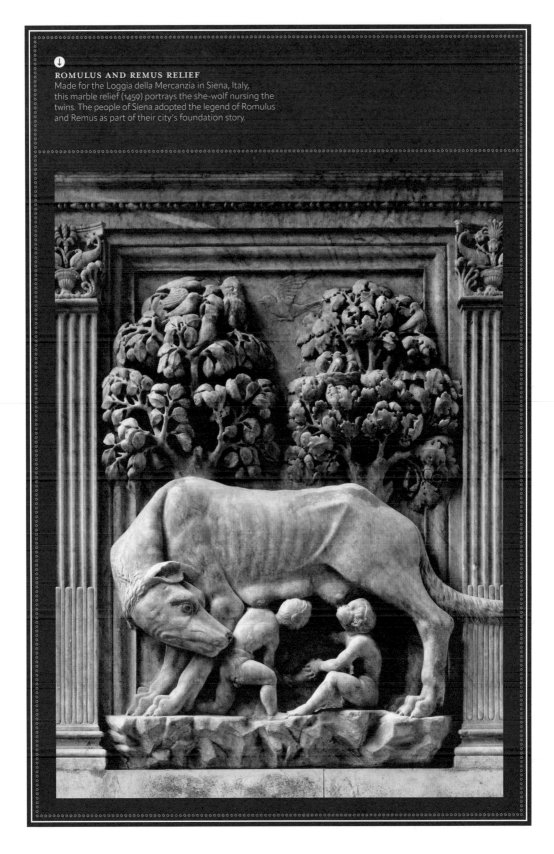

ROMULUS AND REMUS RELIEF
Made for the Loggia della Mercanzia in Siena, Italy,
this marble relief (1459) portrays the she-wolf nursing the
twins. The people of Siena adopted the legend of Romulus
and Remus as part of their city's foundation story.

gave to the legend of Hunahpú and Xbalanqué – shapeshifting trickster twin figures, whose cunning forms an important mythological pattern among other indigenous peoples and oral traditions in the Americas. Hunahpú and Xbalanqué outwit the gods of the underworld and avenge the deaths of their family members. Having triumphed, they ascend over Earth and become dual lights – the sun and the moon.

To visitors of ancient Aztec archaeological sites Quetzalcoatl is often the most recognizable and familiar of all the Aztec gods, and therefore the most human. He is frequently 'twinned' with dog-headed Xolotol – the god of twins but also of the sick and physically malformed. This is common in different societies documented in the Americas, where twin figures are associated with the power of elements – sun and fire, wind and lightning – as well as the human vulnerable, sick and disabled. Again, twins are given a heroic status among these and other myths, while also having a godliness that is imperfect and corruptible.

We learn that ancient societies sought twins as foundational heroes. Imaginative, religious and social practices may use twins in ways that are specific in time and place. But the usefulness of twins remains a compelling feature of those practices, giving twins and twin legends their meaning and power.

Archaeologists of the future may be baffled by the great twin commodities of our times: the bombastic and experimental expressions of twinning created by Hollywood; the vaudevillian twin performers of social media; the industrialized creation and circulation of twin people and data by modern science. They may also prefer to see the similarities rather than the differences – twins still explore the stars as NASA scientists and help people perforate both natural and other worlds as part of the latest bioengineering experiments. Moreover, these future archaeologists, on seeing the heroic twins that populate prehistory, may conclude the twins of this era are also products of political circumstances. Their selection may not be algorithmic, but history has promoted particular twin visions over others. ✿✿

✿✿

HUNAHPÚ AND XBALANQUÉ
A figure of the Mayan twin gods – tricksters, shapeshifters and heroes (c. AD 550–830).

THE TRANSFORMATIONS OF XBALANQUÉ
Mayan vessels depicting the Hero Twin Xbalanqué in various guises (c. AD 600–900).

LORDS ON K'IN LAKAM CHAHK'S THRONE
The figures carved on this Mayan stone throne display intricate symmetries (AD 785).

HERO TWINS AND THE LORDS OF DEATH
Painted on a ceramic cup, the Hero Twins trick the lords of the underworld (c. AD 600–900).

DUAL FIGURES FROM MAYAN RUINS
Stone figures excavated at the Mayan city of Chichén Itzá, located in modern-day Yucatán State, Mexico (c. AD 600–900).

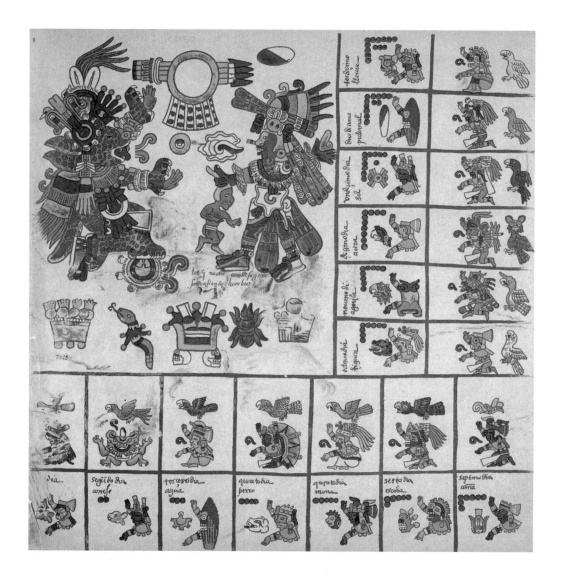

⬆ / ➡

**QUETZALCOATL
AND TEZCATLIPOCA**

The Aztec twin creator gods are seen here in pages from a facsimile of the *Codex Borbonicus* (c. 1520), originally created in the Valley of Mexico. The first section of the codex contains twenty pages, each representing one of the *trecena*, or thirteen-day periods of the 260 days of the Aztec Sacred Year. Each of these pages features a painting of the ruling god or gods and is surrounded by glyphs and deities related to each of the thirteen days. The *Codex Borbonicus* is a single 14-m-long (46 ft) sheet of *amati* (bark) paper.

❊❊ Twins can generate order or disrupt it…. Their conflict may result in the establishment of boundaries … or the disruption of them. ❊❊

John Lash, *Twins and the Double*, 1993

II.   Evil Twins

———————————— ✧ ✧ ————————————

Myths are valuable because they show how twins are usefully ambiguous. In them, twins become diligent artisans, gilding orders of nature and chaos. They are heroic, and the reverse: living embodiments of all that is awful and repellent, horrifying and strange. In turn, twins are violated or discarded. Here, among ancient societies and their religions, twins murder or deserve death.

Twins are asked which is the 'evil twin' – the term given to a menacing tradition, in which one wicked sibling always appears with a more honourable companion. The evil twin is lamplit by a contrasting other. The label propagates a recent and rather more commonplace naughtiness. But the evil twin represents a longer, more ancient dualism, which uses twins as bearers of cosmic wickedness and destruction.

Indigenous American peoples composing the original five nations of Haudenosaunee (People of the Longhouse) – Seneca, Cayuga, Onondaga, Oneida and Mohawk – tell versions of a creation story. Twins are born to the daughter of Sky Woman, called Earth Mother. The first twin is born normally, but the second is born through its mother's side, thus killing her and setting in motion a good twin/bad twin dichotomy. The twins are the source of creative and destructive acts that form Earth's hospitable and hostile environments, beneficial and harmful medicines.[1]

In other mythological traditions, twins murder. In the legends of ancient Egypt, Greece and Rome, we find the gifted Dioscuri, but also Eurytus and Cteatus (named the Moliones or Molionidai, after their mother) – fearsome and powerfully conjoined twins, whose disfigurement is a source of their extraordinary strength. Later accounts see them killed by Heracles, as he avenges the death of his twin brother Iphicles. Fashioning twin gods as heroes is not the only way of dealing with the twin anomaly; another is to imagine them as figures of violence and violent rejection.

Ashamed of being raped by Zeus, Antiope abandons her twins, Amphion and Zethus, and leaves them to die. They go on to found the city of Thebes. The heroic turns to horror. Amphion has his own multiple sets of twins with Niobe. This is a source of great pride, but it enrages the jealous Leto, mother to twins Apollo and Artemis. They defend Leto's honour by killing all of Amphion and Niobe's children – Apollo kills the boys and Artemis kills the girls.[2] There is no happy ending here. In these stories, twins are not cute, desirable or even majestic god figures. They are terrifying and violent.

Zoroastrianism, an ancient Persian religion dominant for more than a thousand years from 600 BC, required primal god figures to be both good (Ahura Mazdā) and evil (Ahriman) – two opposing 'twain spirits', or twin brothers.[3] Some traditions describe and depict evil Ahriman as a literal twin and miscreant incarnate. It is not enough for such figures to *become* evil; they must be so by nature. Just as the newborn Jacob fights Esau over the status of being first born, so Ahriman tears himself

⬅

THE TWIN OCCULT
Twins have often been used in literature, photography and film to unnerve and terrify viewers. In this eerie photograph the twins walking away from the viewer have a ghostly, ethereal quality to them.

out of the womb before his brother. Blood meets soil. Evil takes flesh.[4]

Like heroic and godly stories about twins, murderous or strange twin legends have been reused over generations. The great chronicle of Sri Lanka's Sinhalese founding, *The Mahāvamsa* (*c.* 5th or 6th century), tells the story of Vijaya. His mother leaves a royal household in India and is abducted by a lion. They have twins, a daughter and son. The son kills his lion father and then has sixteen pairs of twins with his mother (Vijaya is one of these). Vijaya's creation required many cultural taboos and social transgressions: sex between animal and human; the murder of father by son; incest between mother and son. Vijaya is not depicted as an intimate to others. He becomes a menace and is expelled from mainland India to the island of Lanka. There, he and his followers cast out demons. Vijaya becomes king and creates a Buddhist haven.[5]

Over centuries, twin legends excite difference and conflict between ethnic and religious groups. The 'stranger king' story, born of bestiality and incest, remains a potent symbol for Sri Lankan Sinhalese nationalists,[6] just as fratricidal twins Romulus and Remus became integral to Mussolini's fascism during the 1920s and 1930s. At the heart of such legends are many experiences of twin fascination, and numerous other feelings for twins and what they represent. Bad king twins shape cultural identities positively and negatively: they steward social practices of intimacy and desire between people, and they sustain violent horror between them.

Although chaos and disorder accompany these twins, ancient philosophers and medical writers attempted to provide orderly reasons for the existence of twins. The Hippocratic texts (5th to 4th century BC) state that twins occur because a woman's uterus has two parts and when the seed from both parents is 'abundant and strong'. Aristotle (384–322 BC) also considered twin births to be created from biological excess – great quantities of seed. For Aristotle, what is commonly observed reflects a purpose. Nature has an orderliness or 'teleology' that is guided by observed frequency. This led Aristotle to view twins as 'monstrous' and contrary to reproductive norms. They are a corruption, like other physical deformities. 'The reason why the parts may be multiplied contrary to nature is the same as the cause of the birth of twins,' wrote Aristotle, 'For the reason exists already in the embryo, whenever more material gathers than is required by the nature of the part. The result is then that either one of its parts is larger than the others, as a finger or hand or foot or any of the other extremities or limbs; or again if the embryo is cleft there may come into being more than one, as eddies do in rivers ...'.[7] His explanations of excess are not only biological. They touch on how societies are organized and regulated. His treatise on reproduction explains that twins also occur when women have multiple sexual partners: women who are raped or women who have sexual affairs outside of their marriages.

In Western scientific traditions, twins were looked upon in terms of different mechanical and moral orders. Sexual difference was pivotal to how the strangeness of twins was managed and explained. Anatomical doctrines of a two-part uterus evolved, and became seven-celled by the 12th century. Italian medics popularized the idea that the uterus had three chambers on the left for the development of females, three on the right for the males, and another in the middle for intersex people (hermaphrodites).[8] Such ideas drew on the work of the highly influential medieval medical thinker Ibn Sina (980–1037,

❶ AMPHION AND ZETHUS
Wall painting in the House of the Vettii, Pompeii. It depicts the twins killing their aunt Dirce by tying her to a bull (*c.* AD 62).

❷ AHURA MAZDĀ
The good god, whose twin evil spirit is Ahriman, is shown in this relief at Naqsh-e-Rostam, Iran, anointing Emperor Ardashir I (AD 226–242).

➡ TWINS AND MULTIPLES
A page from *De Animalibus*, a work of natural philosophy on twins and multiples. It shows a woman carrying twenty-eight foetuses (1300s).

➡ DOUBLE PANNIERS
Babies are depicted being carried in double panniers across the base of this page taken from *The Romance of Alexander* (*c.* 1338–1410).

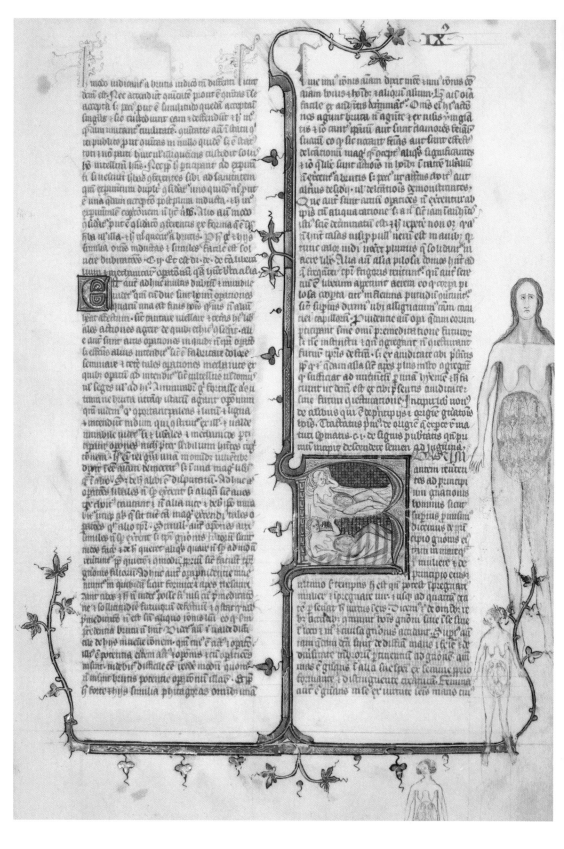

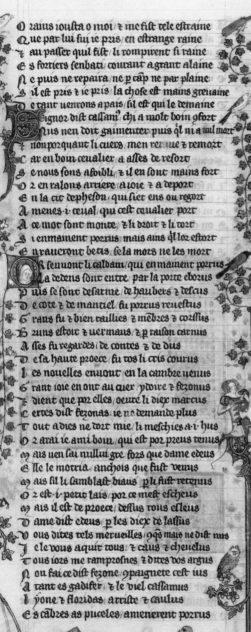

O raius iousta o moi / z me fist tele estraine
Que par lui fui ie pris / en estrange raine
z au passer quil fist / li rompirent si raine
E s fortiers senbati courant agrant alaine
N e puis ne repaira / ne p car ne par plaine
S il est pris z ie pris / la chose est mains greuaine
E tant uenrons apais / sil est qui le demaine
D ignoz dist cassam? chi a molt boin gsort
S us nen doit gaimenter / puis qil ni a nul mort
N onporquant li cuers / men reuiue z remort
C ar en boin ceualier a asses de resort
S enous sons afoibli / z il en sont mains fort
O z en ralons arriere / a ioie z a deport
E n la cit depheson / qui siet ens ou regort
A menes i ceual / qui cest ceualier port
A ce mot sont monte / z li droit z li tort
S i enmainent porrus / mais ains qil loz estort
E nrauront betis / se la mors ne les mort

R senuont li caldain / qui en mainent porrus
L a dedens sont entre / par la porte eborus
p uis se sont desarme / de haubers z descus
D e cote z de mantiel / fu porrus reuestus
G rans fu z bien taillies z mebres z corssus
B runs estoit z uermaus / z p raison carnus
A sses fu regardes / de contes z de dus
D e sa haute proece / fu tos li cris courus
L es nouelles enuont / en la cambre uenus
G rant ioie en ont au cuer / ydoire z sezonus
z dient que por elles / oeure li dieux marcus
C ertes dist sezonas ie ne demande plus
T out a dieu ne dort mie / li meschies a i hus
O z arai ie ami boin / qui est por preus tenus
m ais uen sai nullui gre / fors que dame edeus
E lle le motria / anchois que fust uenus
m ais sil li camblast biaus / p li fust retenus
O z est i petit lais / por ce mest escheus
m ais il est de proece / dessus tous esleus
D ame dist edeus / p les diex de lassus
V ous dites tels merueilles / que mais ne dist nus
J e le vous aquit tous / z caus z cheuelus
T ous iors me ramprosnes / z dites vos argus
S on faice dist sezone / gpaignete cest ius
A tant es gadifer / z le viel cassamus
J yone z floridas / arriste z caulus
E s cabres as puceles / amenerent porrus

L es puceles se sont / tantost leuees sus
z iel z cortoisement / ont les grus recueillus
C ascune prent le sien / puis serassient ius
L or prisonnier porron / assirent dedessus

Comment porrus fint plouuer et
armes des armes a les dames

E n la chambre uenus
repairierent li gre
D esarme de lor armes
de robes bien pare
A uoec eaus amenerent
lor prisonnier porre
L es puceles li ont / molt grant honor porte
p or le grant bien de lui / quon en auoit conte
q uelles ont veu / des murs sus le fosse
S i auoient de lui / veoir molt desire
F ezonias laissist / de roste son coste
p ar mi les dois le prent / si la bel aparle
S ire dist la pucele / molt maura huy greue
L i trauaus perilleus quaues huy endure
m ale gent sont villain / z mal auise
S e trop ne fussies preus / mal vous fust engtre
J l vous euissent mort / occhis z decope
m ais treshaute proece / vous en a deliure
D ame ce dist porrus / qui a i poi pense
V ous dites cortoisie / z vostre uolente
m ais se li viex preudons ou tant a de bonte
N e meuist secouru / il meuissent tue
N reche dist cassam? se ia aie sante

⬇

MATER MATUTA I
Tufa sculpture of the goddess Mater Matuta (400–100 BC),
who was linked to a fertility cult. It was found in the
Fondo Patturelli sanctuary, near Capua, Italy.

↓

MATER MATUTA II
Tufa sculpture of Mater Matuta (400–300 BC) from the
Fondo Patturelli sanctuary, near Capua, Italy. The name
'Mater Matuta' translates as 'mother of dawn'.

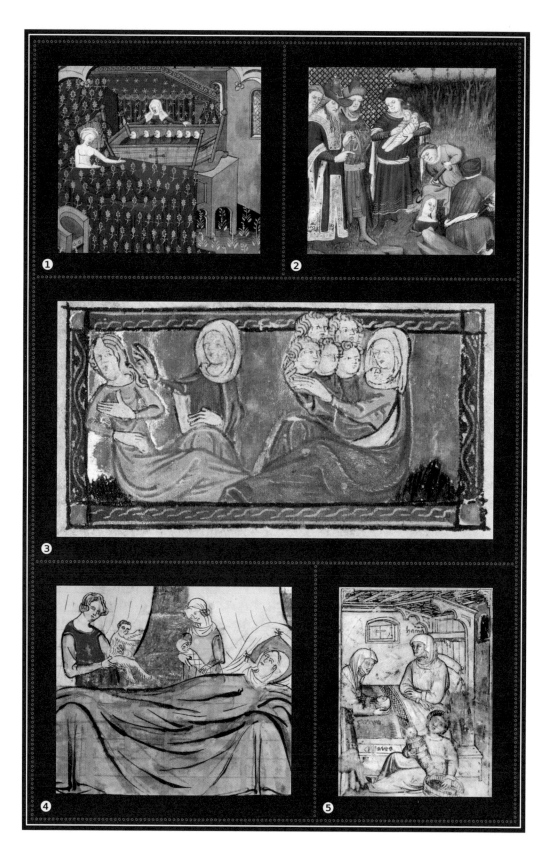

also known as Avicenna), who agreed with Greek authorities that twins were made when there was an abundance of semen. He added that twinning required semen to be split into different parts, brought on by the motion of sexual pleasure.[9] Following Ibn Sina, 14th-century philosopher John of Jandun (c. 1286–1328) argued that twins and other deformations are related to physical pleasure: 'It is dangerous that the female moves during sexual intercourse in the way prostitutes are reputed to do, because if at such moment they would conceive, they could generate an awful two-headed monster.'[10] For Christian monks and scholars, multiple births were a threat to orders of gender and sexuality. The careful management of twins – their lives and the meaning of their lives – could help to safeguard biological and spiritual knowledge.

European medieval folksong and storytelling traditions also dramatized the opinion that twinning was a calamitous event, a sinful and incriminating display of erotic desire and sexual deviancy.[11] Moralistic romance stories saw countless fictional women being accused of adultery for having twin children. At the beginning of some of these stories, a woman would become pregnant with twins and her neighbour would accuse her of having sex with two men. Then the neighbour – whose point of view everyone had accepted – also becomes pregnant with twins. She knows she will also be under suspicion, and so abandons one twin and keeps the other. The stories develop, and eventually the twins are recognized, reunited and married. But the entertainment begins with a simple association between twins and sexual immorality.

Conjoined twins in pre-modern times had very high mortality rates, as did their mothers. They were considered monsters, prodigious signs – messages from God that required careful theological and scientific interpretation. Conjoined twins were born in Florence, Italy, around 1317. Years later, the poet and scholar Petrarch (1304–74) recalled his family being sent a picture of the children, and his father urging him to remember the birth, to pass on the story and ensure the sign can be understood by future generations.[12] Until the early 1600s, these meticulous records and reports of conjoined births circulated internationally.[13] Churches had sculptures added to their buildings, and religious and civic leaders linked them with celestial events, famine, flood, earthquakes and drought to divine their meaning.

Having little alternative to destitution, conjoined twins of later centuries toured as entertainers and were the subjects of popular ballads or woodcut images. From the 1700s onwards, moral worries about conjoined people gradually gave way to an increasingly professional and medicalized interest. Prodigious monsters that once straddled thresholds between the natural and supernatural realms also guided scientific and religious ideas about what divided natural and artificial life. Natural histories, then and now, captured conjoined twins in a pathologically abnormal category of bodily difference – their biographies subsumed by the medical 'case' – and treated them

---

☆ ☆

SEVEN IN A CRADLE
Detail of an illuminated manuscript showing a mother with seven children, created in Rouen, France (c. 1445).

ROMULUS AND REMUS
Illustration from a manuscript depicting the birth of the Roman twins and the killing of their mother, Rhea Silvia (c. 1415).

QUINTUPLETS
Illustration from *Der naturenbloeme* (1271–72) of quintuplets who were said to have lived for eight years.

QUADRUPLETS OF DORDRECHT, 1621
This painting of the quadruplets born to Cornelia Jans of Dordrecht, who died an hour after being born, reclining on a pillow and wearing a death shirt and rosemary wreath, and Pieter, Jannetje and Maria alive in swaddling clothes. They were baptized three days later but died within a week.

JACOB AND ESAU
This miniature from Guyart des Moulins' *Bible Historiale* (1291–95) depicts the birth of twins Jacob and Esau.

PEREZ AND ZERAH
Biblical twins Perez and Zerah are depicted newly swaddled by the midwife in this miniature (1390–1400).

PIETER · DE · 1.
Æ · SVÆ · 5 · DÃ
EN · 5 · VREN

IANNETTE · DE · 2.
Æ · SVÆ · 3 · DÃ · EN · 15 ·

. SIET, DE KINDEREN ZYN EEN, GHAVE DES HEER
ENDE DE VRVCHT DES LYFS IS EEN GHESCHEN·
PSALM · C · XXVII ·

MARIA · DE · 4
Æ · SVÆ · 3 · DA̅

ELISABET · DE · 3
Æ · SVÆ · I · ½ · VR

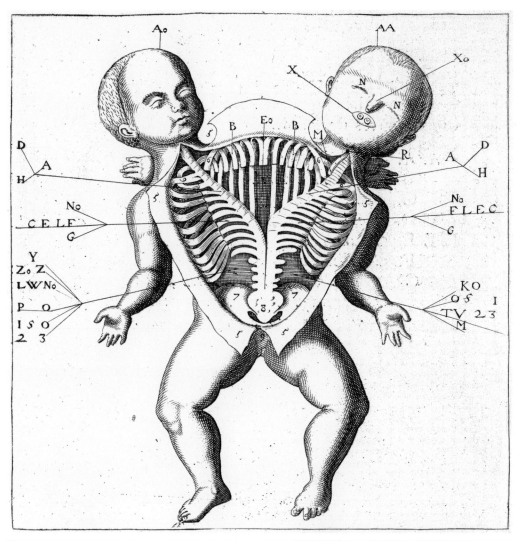

STUDY OF 'MONSTERS'
Plates from *De Monstruorum
Causis, Natura et Differentiis*
(1616). Fortunio Liceti (1577–1657)
meticulously documented
cases of human and animal
'monsters', arguing that not
all were supernatural beings.

✧✧ ... the parents, the midwife,
and the parish priest had to
determine if a monstrous baby
... was one person or two. ✧✧

Lorraine Daston and Katherine Park,
Wonders and the Orders of Nature, 1998

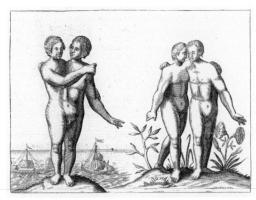
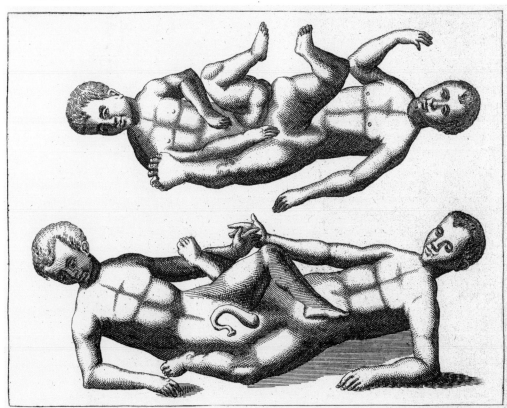

> ✢✢ **Crossing over from the archaic world, however, double-bodied oracles have spoken less of Nature than of the unnatural.** ✢✢
>
> Hillel Schwartz, *The Culture of the Copy*, 1996

as deviations from other twins, themselves deviations from the 'norm' of single birth.

The history of separating conjoined twins communicates changing ideas about individual and bodily autonomy. Some argue the practice of dividing conjoined twins began in AD 945 with conjoined twin boys in Constantinople, where one boy died and his surviving brother lived just three days. Surgeries that resulted in the survival of both twins would come centuries later, with conjoined girls born near Basel, Switzerland, in 1689.[14]

The shame and embarrassment of having twins could be greater than the pain felt when abandoning them. Twins have been left for different reasons.[15] Into the 19th and 20th centuries, twins were ritually abandoned. Fears that twins are abnormal, kill the sick, pollute or damage livestock and crops, arise from adultery, are cursed and embody evil are just some of the reasons that twin infanticide has been documented in Europe, Africa, South Asia and the Americas. In the last century, the killing of twins has circulated in the news and other media in geopolitical and colonial contexts. Church missionaries, colonial officials, medics and anthropologists have responded to twin infanticide and sought both meaning and opportunities to change the values of colonized societies. Some of the first Christian mission stations in West Africa were positioned where mothers abandoned twins and other unwanted children. White Europeans considered themselves saviours to these children and converted their mothers. Practices are time sensitive and complex, however. In the 18th and 19th centuries, twins born to the Yoruba in West Africa were an unequivocal sign that the mother was morally

wicked. Twins were viewed as a supernatural curse. Their mothers were accused of having sex with spirits, and she and her children were exiled or killed.[16] There is some evidence that neighbouring Ekiti, Bunu and Ondo peoples practised twin infanticide in the early parts of the 20th century. Oyo Yoruba people are thought to have changed their customs when they came into contact with neighbours who experienced good fortune when twins were born.[17] Alternative traditions emerged and came to replace practices of infanticide, including those that celebrated twins as a special gift from God, and treated them with care and reverence as a deity in miniature. More recently, and with the increased influence of Christianity, Islam and modern medicine, the cultural requirement to venerate twins and celebrate twin rites has lessened. Twins are finding new forms of cultural 'ordinariness' – further reinterpreted and no longer seen as fearful abominations.[18]

Twins participate in systems of social classification that are underpinned by single-born conceptions of nature and order. They give human form to social and moral anomalies. The control and regulation of twins give legitimacy to the powerful. Twins also provide monstrously exciting, evasive, provoking and awe-inspiring characters in foundational and other mythological stories. Twins may fascinate, but only because humans put them at the edge of human power, reason and control. ✢✢

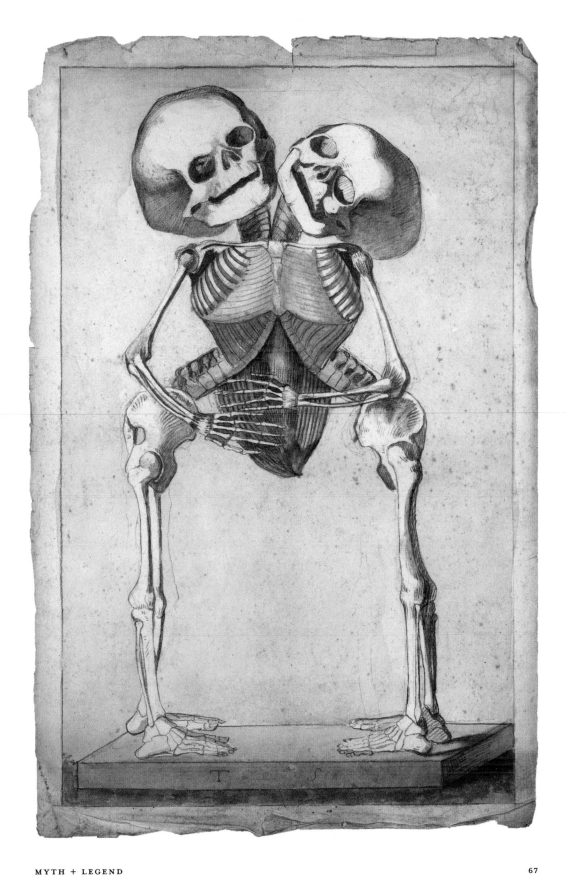

↓
CONJOINED BABIES
This illustration of conjoined twins was included
with a report on birth accidents and deaths by Robert
Bland (1730–1816) presented at The Royal Society in 1781.
A midwife and physician, Robert Bland took a scientific
interest in 'monstrous productions'.

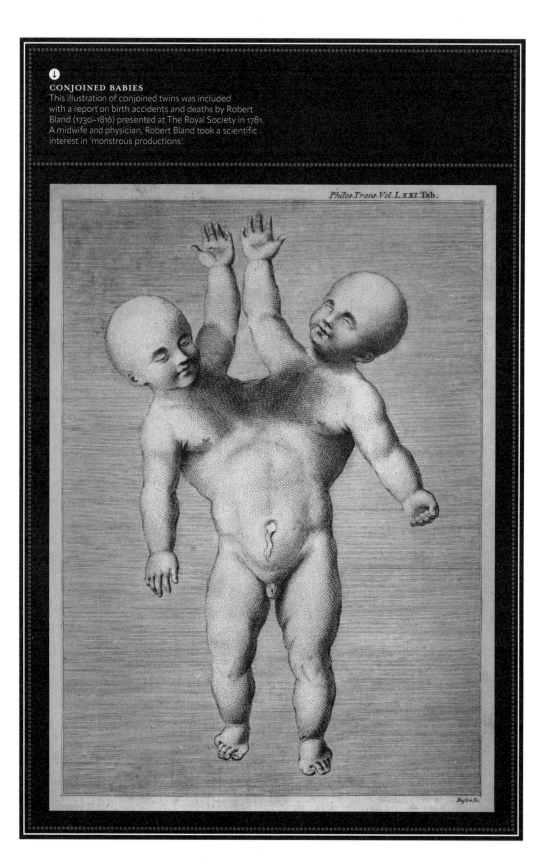

Philos.Trans.Vol.LXXI.Tab.

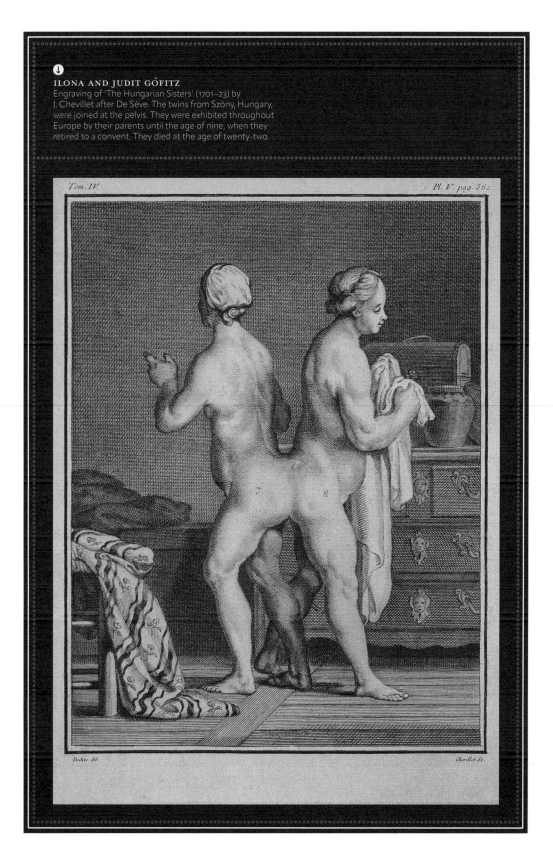

ILONA AND JUDIT GÓFITZ
Engraving of 'The Hungarian Sisters' (1701–23) by
J. Chevillet after De Sève. The twins from Szöny, Hungary,
were joined at the pelvis. They were exhibited throughout
Europe by their parents until the age of nine, when they
retired to a convent. They died at the age of twenty-two.

De Seve del.

Chevillet Sc.

☆☆One of the odd accidents that can occur only with identical twins is their failure in some cases to separate completely ... ☆☆

Amran Scheinfeld, *Twins and Supertwins*, 1967

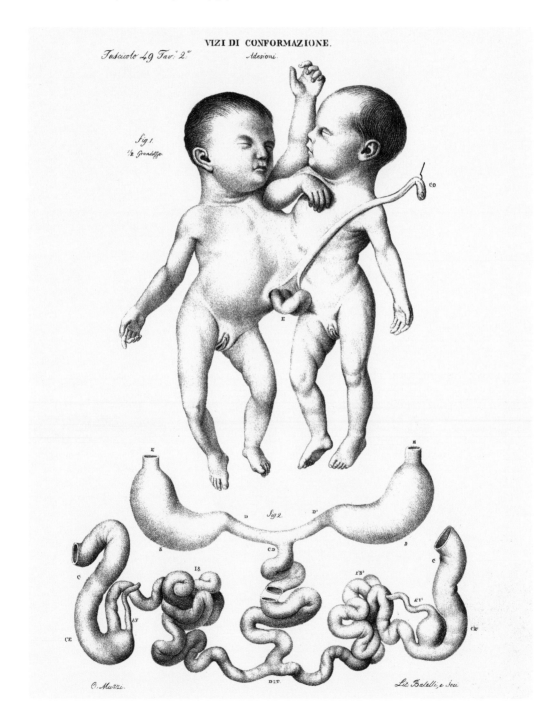

← **FORMATION OF CONJOINED TWINS**
Plate from an 18th-century volume showing that conjoined twins share one placenta during pregnancy.

↓ **CONJOINED TWINS — ANATOMICAL PLATE**
Second plate from scientific volume illustrating the distribution of the internal organs of conjoined twins.

→ **RADHIKA AND DUDHIKA**
Photograph of Dr Eugène Doyen separating the twins in 1902 after Dudhika became ill. Radhika lived for another twenty-one months.

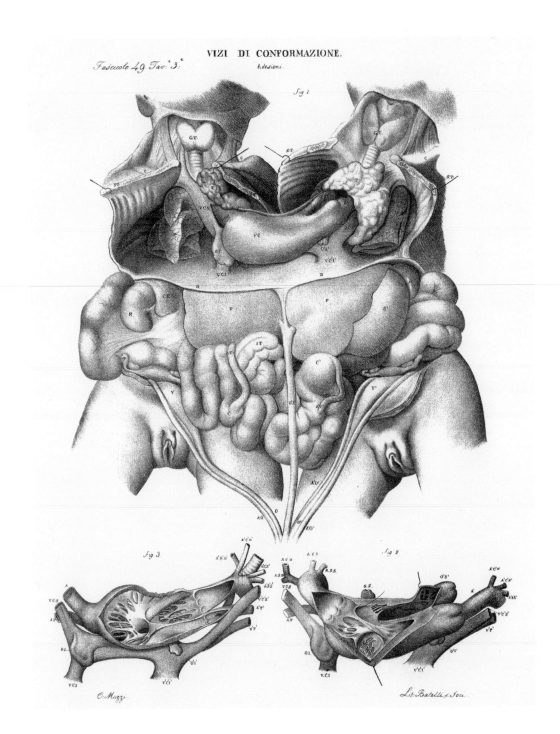

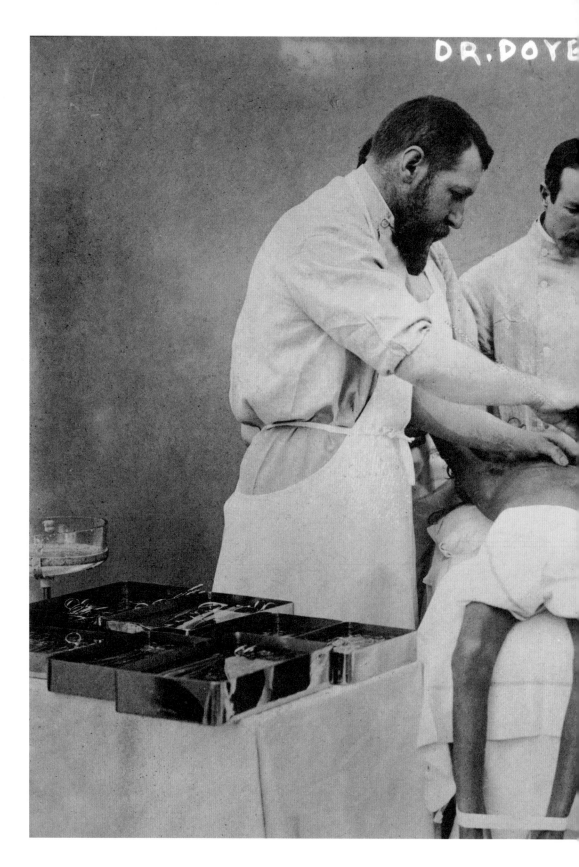

DR. DOYE

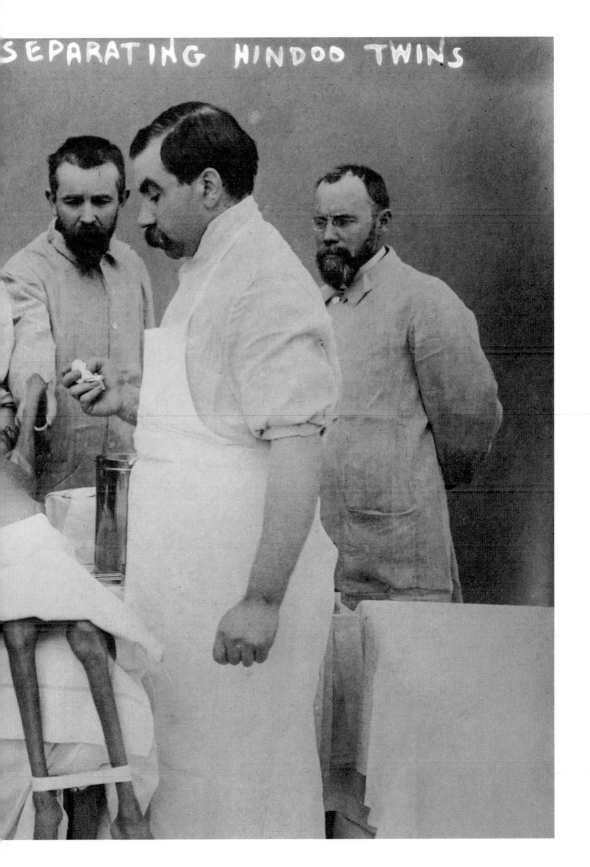

SEPARATING HINDOO TWINS

III. Twin Spirits

✿ ✿

Responses to the birth of twin people in parts of Africa, Asia and the Americas have been discussed and debated for centuries. They illustrate a paradox about twinning and the social existence of twins. Twins are often treated as two persons that occupy the social position of one being. They are alike, and for that reason different from others. In some societies they are seen as people suffused with one spirit or two, one heart with two bodies, as some Indigenous Americans have reported. For this reason, according to British anthropologist Victor Turner (1920–83), who lived among the Ndembu people of Zambia in the 1960s, twins are 'a source of classificatory embarrassment ... at once more human and less than human'.[1]

Cultures respond to this paradox in different ways by managing twin identities with local rites and rituals. Until the mid- to late-19th century, twins born to the Yoruba peoples, an ethnic group now concentrated in modern-day Nigeria, Benin and Togo, were viewed as a spiritual disasters. Infanticide was widely practised. Oyo Yorubans in what is now southeastern Nigeria found fortune in twin births, changed their practices, and abomination turned to celebration by the 20th century. Gradually twins became viewed as sacred throughout Yorubaland. They were believed to bring fortune to parents and communities. Treating twins with veneration and respect was believed to protect and preserve the communities. Twins were given praise names, special medicines, foods and shrines to respect a shared spirit.

Anthropological reports of the 20th century document Yoruban people saying twins are 'born of monkeys', whose meat the twins and their parents were forbidden to eat. Here was one of many spiritual connections. Another was the connection between twin pairs, which was said to be so strong that should one die, the other was believed to be in danger. Traditional craftsmen created small, devotional memorial statues called *ere ibeji* (*ere* meaning 'sacred image', *ibi* meaning 'born' and *eji* meaning 'two'). These statues were ceremoniously cared for and carried by mothers or surviving twins, to respect the memory of the departed and safeguard the survivor.

Memorial carvings or substitutes, such as vessels, figures and photographs, are found in modern Niger, Benin, Mali and Sierra Leone, and in different parts of the Black Atlantic.[2] In modern Cuba, Haiti and Brazil, religious customs have adapted and evolved. For Candomblé practitioners in Brazil, the twin traditions of West Africa combine with Catholic ones, especially those linked to the martyred twin saints Cosmas and Damian. Their saints' day, 26 September, is a time to celebrate *erês*, or childlike spirits.[3] Haitian Vodou also venerates and celebrates twins, called the Marasa. They are central to a pantheon of *lwa*, or ancestor spirits, derived from Yoruba, Fon/Ewe, Kongo and other African customs and religions, syncretized with European Catholicism and freemasonry. Although the Marasa may bring healing, they

TWIN MASK
Belonging to the Baule peoples of the Bandama River region, the twin mask would be worn to honour someone's artistic double or namesake.

also cause pain and suffering if they are not cared for and respected. They bring both blessings and a threat.[4] What is distinctive in Haitian Vodou, as in other diaspora twin cultures, is how the meaning and experience of twinning gathers still-living twins and dead, cosmic and ancestral twin spirits.

Twins have been imagined as gods, demi-gods and monsters in different locations and at different times. Their conception, birth, competition or collaboration are related to a variety of non-human beings, animals and spirits. For those who are not twins and happen to be invested in understanding them, twin people around the world have tended to be seen as a community that experiences the extremes of sameness and its opposite. Paradoxically, we may observe striking cultural differences in how twins are valued at different times, in different parts of the world, yet this comparison requires twins to have enduring qualities or experiences in common. Understanding the extent to which this drama is a natural or cultural phenomenon has been fundamental to the modern, scientific analysis of human society. As the 20th century progressed, this became another reason why twins were made to walk a stage designed to explain who (and what) we are.

Attempts to describe 'traditional' cultures have frequently seized on how different societies distinguish human and animal behaviour. Dogon elders of Mali in the 1950s reported that twins were animals: snakes, lizards, chameleons and other species. Throughout the 20th century, associations between twins and snakes were declared to European colonial agents, missionaries, anthropologists and others. Twins of the Ubangian region have been seen as powerful, dangerous and ambiguous people among the fifty or so ethnic groups living in the middle of Africa, between the Republic of the Congo and the Central African Republic. Here, too, twins are compared to snakes. These animal comparisons are a common part of different African belief systems, but it is often the work of outsiders, especially anthropologists, to make comparisons between regions.

In traditional Japanese society the mothers of twins were called *chikushô bara*, or animal uterus,[5] and in Bali, during the early 20th century, lower-caste parents of twins aroused 'a deep-lying feeling that to bear more than one child at a time was to have children as animals do, in litters'.[6] Indigenous American scholar Barbara Alice Mann (b. 1947, Ohio Bear Clan Seneca) argued that understanding matched sets of elements and animals is key to the interdependence and 'iconic twinships' of indigenous philosophy in North America. Evaluating points of comparison is a product of a more abstract desire for cultural patterns of similarity and difference. It is often in this practice of comparison that European ideas of nationhood and population emerge as the containers in which different 'kinds' of twins are placed.

European responses to twin traditions in various cultures have travelled via old colonial pathways, which have served as points of access and extraction – initially through Christian missionary work and colonial administration and later thanks to the formation of social anthropology as a professional field that seeks to understand and compare cultures. Since twins appeared numerically distributed across European

SAINTS COSMAS AND DAMIAN
In this 1495 painting – *A Verger's Dream* – attributed to the Master of Los Balbases, the Arabian-born twin physicians perform a miraculous, inter-racial leg transplant.

❶ BRACELET
Made of ivory, wood and coconut shells, this bracelet is from the Yoruba kingdom Owo.

❹ BRONZE AGE IDOL
Marble twin figure found at Beycesultan, an archaeological site in Turkey (*c.* 3000 BC).

❷ DOUBLE MASK
Made to wear at a Yoruban Gelede festival to celebrate fertility and motherhood.

❺ TWIN FIGURES
Wooden statues made by Igbo craftsmen, indigenous to southeastern Nigeria (1900s).

❸ DOUBLE PENDANT
These gold bat-headed twin pendants originate from the Chiriquí province (1000–1500).

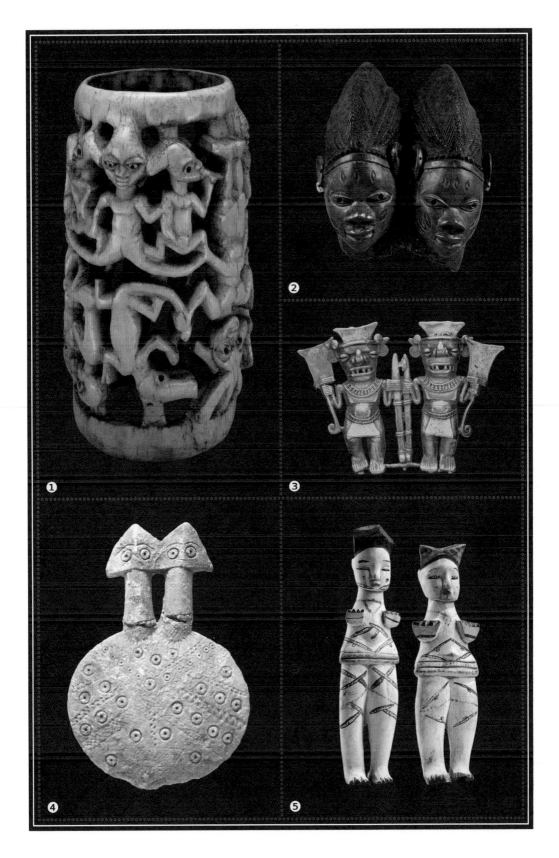

categories of the natural and divine, spiritual and animal, individual and social, twins around the world have been seen as talismanic figures – people whose existence reflects the cultural specificity of a given social reality. Practices of European comparison and Western understandings of similarity and difference continue to be tested against twins in this historical context.

As British anthropologist E. E. Evans-Pritchard (1902–73) discovered when living among the Nuer people of South Sudan during the 1930s, the ambiguous and colonial encounters that Europeans had with twins could have a lasting impact. He observed that for the Nuer 'twins form the closest possible human relationship'. The Nuer also told him that 'a twin is not a person, he is a bird'.[7] Evans-Pritchard and fellow anthropologists were perplexed. Were twins really not people? Were twins equivalent to birds? Or were they *like* birds in terms of shared characteristics, including shared characteristics with God or spirits?[8] This debate preoccupied the profession for many years. Studies of likeness between twins, animals and spirits, and between groups of twins in diverse parts of the world, have made twin people cultural listening posts or 'monitoring instruments' in the quest to understand how human cultures are organized.[9]

Human twins remain unusual and uncommon in most cultures. Again, this rarity is felt according to many systems of comparison. For example, modern Western biology recognizes that the creation of monozygotic (identical) twins is a rare event in other mammals. The nine-banded armadillo is the only other creature that produces twins in a similar way: one fertilized egg develops into separate, genetically alike individuals. Western biology creates comparative taxonomies of similarity that have gained a powerful influence in a relatively short period of time. As with all human artefacts, modern tribes of scientists use categories that must also join a history of sorting and separation, techniques used to distinguish different twins.

In white European and settler colonial North American societies, 'traditional' or indigenous knowledges are reclassified as 'folklore' and stripped of credibility. Yet classic 19th-century narrative traditions of Western literature produced 'the double' or doppelgänger in part to handle the incredible strangeness of dual persons at once more and less than human. The tales of E. T. A. Hoffmann (1776–1822), Charlotte Brontë (1816–55), Dostoevsky (1821–81) and Robert Louis Stevenson (1850–94) created such weird and paranoid fictions because they portray individuals confronted, haunted and sometimes hunted by another person who is identical to them, who first affirms and then threatens protagonists. When twins are conflated with this tradition they are also symbiotically and existentially connected. They are made threatening for being living apertures upon a kind of spiritual chaos and connectivity, on a spiritualism that can be far removed from the universal Christian principle of spiritual sameness and material difference. These fictions achieve something uniquely uncanny for the way they control and contain mysticism: '... a flickering sense (but not conviction) of something supernatural'.[10] In such a divided worldview, scientific modernity is haunted by a double

that is of its own making – the unexplained phenomena that lurk at the thresholds of what can be known and measured. If ethnographic understandings of different twin cultures have catalogued the role of the spirit in the lives of colonized and formally colonized peoples, racializing twin cultures that do not conform to Western scientific practices and principles, then it is important to observe those mechanisms of repression at work in the industrialized metropoles of Europe and North America.

The world's twins are not valued equally. Changing rites of thought, feeling and belief evolve in time and place – set in dynamic relations with the practices we use to observe, measure and describe what twins do. Twins have become some of the most discussed and studied human beings on the planet. They assist us in grasping hold of things unseen; they appear to answer questions related to the most intangible and mysterious and important phenomena. But a sense of history – and justice – requires us to pay cautious attention to how the meaning of twins is made. Collectively, twins have rarely been consulted about their status as tools or 'monitoring instruments'. Universalizing debates have invited or coerced twins to give up their minds, bodies and spirits to science.

Traditional belief systems are never static. What is known of them is updated and revised. Understandings of ancient and modern religion – their relationship to spiritual beliefs, secular categories and scientific practices – remain deeply concerned with how people are split or form different kinds of whole. Twin myths also inspire modern and futuristic visions of change and emancipation. The ancestor spirits of the Dogon people of Mali are twin deities called Nommo (or Nummo). Aboard their ship, the Nommo ascend with thunder and fire to the stars, where elders say they circulate the star Sirius. Although the authenticity of these cosmic creation stories is sometimes doubted – they were told to European anthropologists under specific conditions – they also informed generations of artists and writers. Nommo are key to speculative Afrofuturist visions of solidarity and hope, autonomy and resistance – a mode of social and technological belonging. This sense of a future is tied intimately with continuity and twin company. As African American scholar Marilyn Houlberg (1939–2012) learnt from a Vodou practitioner in Haiti: 'The twins walk with all nations from Africa … twins walk with all nations in the world.'[11] ✧✧

✧ ✧

❶

ERE IBEJI FIGURES 1
Sculptured out of wood these twin female figures are from the workshop of Ibuke Compound, Oyo Yoruban peoples (19th or 20th century).

❷

ERE IBEJI FIGURES 2
Made from wood and glass, these twin female commemorative figures are Yoruban, from Kisi near Old Oyo, Nigeria (20th century).

❸

ERE IBEJI FIGURES 3
This male and female pair of sculptured figures, created by the Yoruban people from wood and adorned with beads, represent twins (20th century).

❹

ERE IBEJI FIGURES 4
Male and female Yoruban figures from the cult of Shango. Adorned with shells and beads, the figures were created when one twin died (20th century).

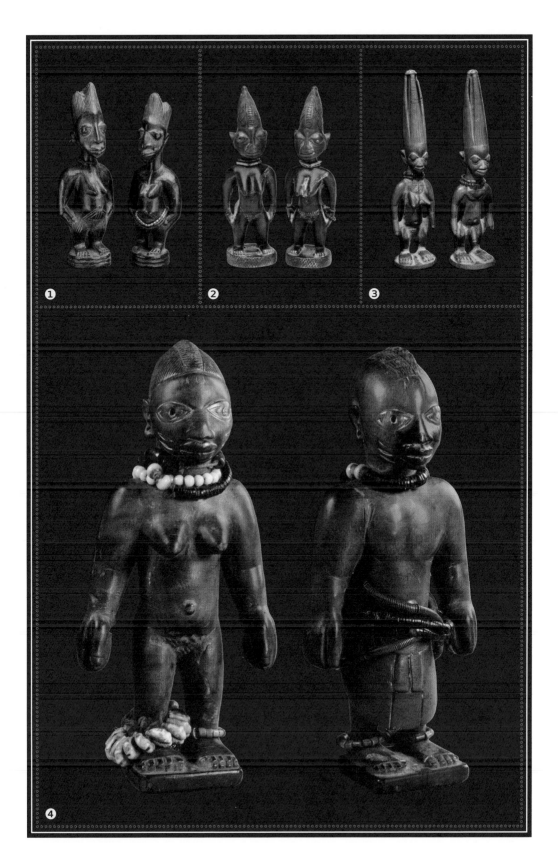

MASK OF JANUS
This 20th-century mask was made by the Senufo peoples of West Africa. The name 'Janus' – the two-headed Roman god of beginnings – is a colonial attribution.

ZODIAC ILLUSTRATION
An illustration of the Gemini twins, or al-Gawāz, taken from the first section of the *Kitāb al-Bulhān* or 'Book of Wonders' (1390), a composite manuscript in Arabic of divinatory works compiled by Abd al-Hasan Al-Isfahani and bound in Baghdad during the reign of Jalayirid Sultan Ahmad (1382–1410). The Arabic manuscript is composed of astrological, astronomical and geomantic texts together with full-page illustrations.

PORTRAIT OF TWINS
This oil painting depicts two female twins wearing almost identical outfits, painted by an unknown Iranian artist in the late 18th to early 19th century.

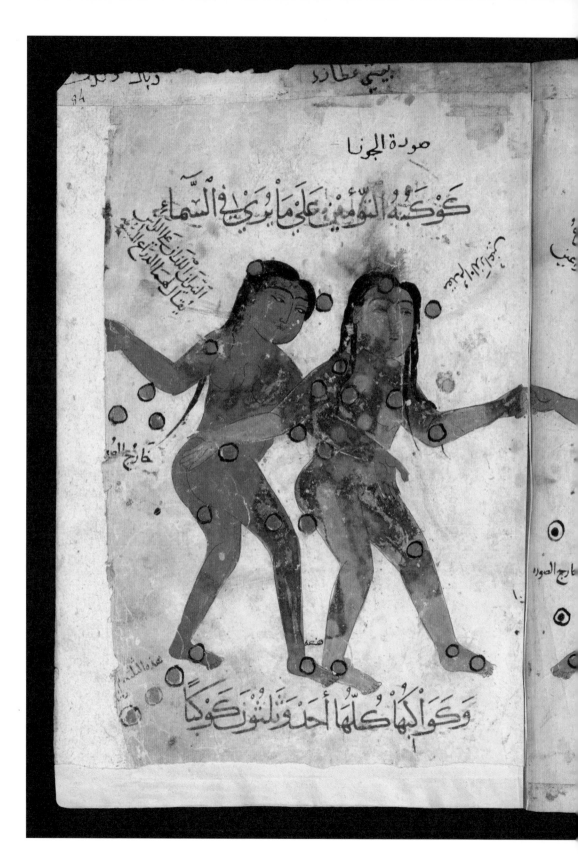

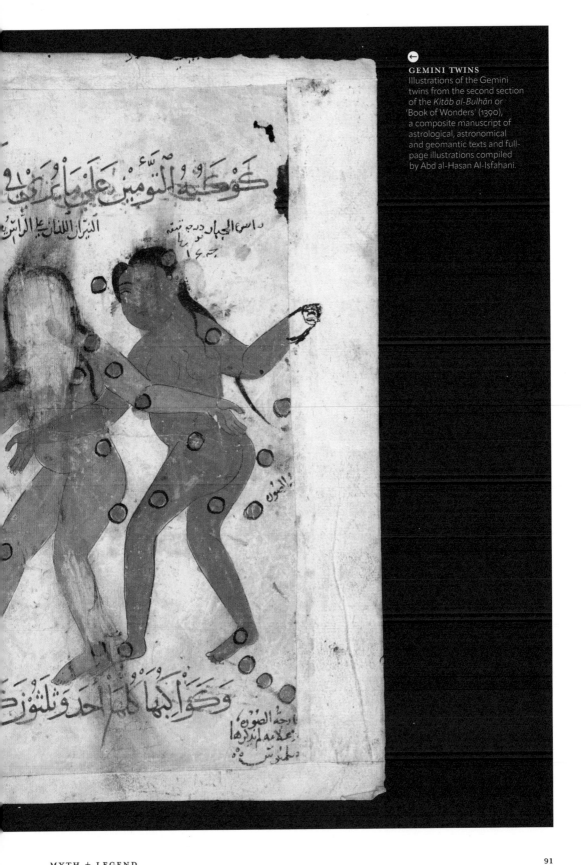

←

GEMINI TWINS
Illustrations of the Gemini twins from the second section of the *Kitāb al-Bulhān* or 'Book of Wonders' (1390), a composite manuscript of astrological, astronomical and geomantic texts and full-page illustrations compiled by Abd al-Hasan Al-Isfahani.

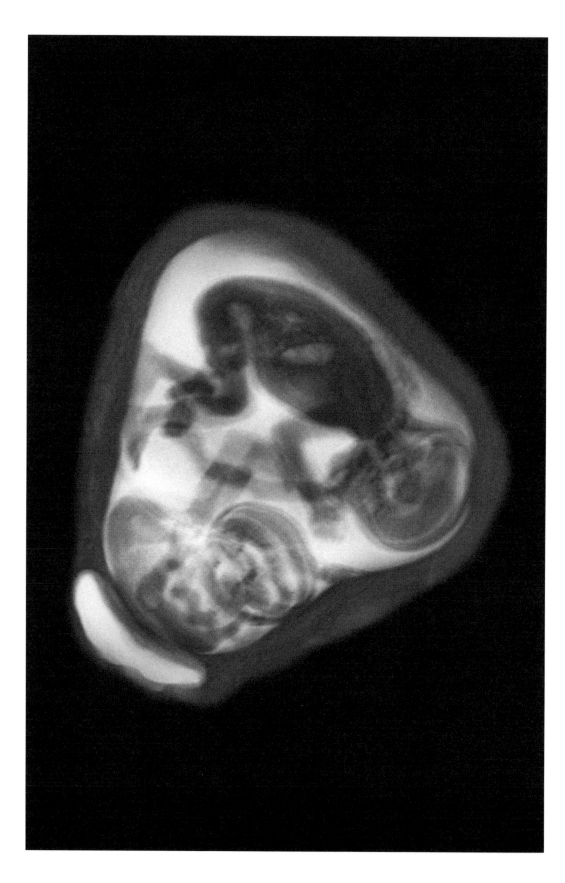

PART TWO

✳ ✳

SCIENCE + PROGRESS
SCIENCE + PROGRESS

✳ ✳

БУДЬТЕ ВСЕГДА ЗДОРОВЫ!

IV. Nature *and* Nurture

✾ ✾

As we have seen, twins have been treated as figures of both virtue and vice. And they have been used to illustrate many transition points between these extremes. The science of the Victorian era was no less interested in twins as an opportunity for making sense of human life – a way of seeing the unseen and testing the unknown. Technical methods emerged for comparing and valuing different people. These were applied in the violent quest to control domestic and colonial territories, populations and resources. Measuring differences and similarities between human groups also expanded the influence of the human sciences, such as anthropology, psychology, sociology and statistics, in public life. Seeds of a twin science were sown in the 19th century, and they gradually grew into an industry, empowered to define every aspect of human health and behaviour.

One man came to symbolize the Victorian energy and enthusiasm for measurement. Francis Galton (1822–1911) was born to a prosperous and highly educated English family. He was distantly related to Charles Darwin (1809–82) and shared the privileges of upper-middle-class society. Among his many scientific achievements, he created the statistical practice of correlation and regression – finding numerical patterns between variables and demonstrating statistical norms.[1] By measuring different characteristics between parents and their children, his biometric science aimed to demonstrate normal distributions within a population. By doing this, he was able to develop the idea of regression towards averages for particular traits.

Galton was particularly concerned with how talents pass between family members. He dedicated many years to testing the intellectual superiority of his white, male and wealthy peers. After formative years spent in West Africa, he returned to London to advocate a racism common to the imperial British. For Galton and other race scientists, the moral, mental and physical superiority of rich white Europeans was a natural state of affairs. This was best shown objectively in statistics.

Success in science combines impactful evidence, reproducible methods and the complex art of public relations. In his essay 'The History of Twins, as a Criterion of the Relative Powers of Nature and Nurture' (1875), Galton combined all three 'to weigh in just scales the effects of Nature and Nurture, and to ascertain their respective shares in framing the disposition and intellectual ability of men'.[2] He sent questionnaires to pairs of twins and received around eighty responses. He categorized twins as 'strongly alike', 'moderately alike' or 'extremely dissimilar', and then calculated how twin pairs tended to grow more or less alike over their lifetimes. The phrase 'nature and nurture' is now familiar, but it was Galton who furnished it with scientific importance and a certain

MRI OF TWIN FOETUSES
Coloured magnetic resonance imaging (MRI) scan of 32-week-old twin male foetuses. The placenta, in blue, can be seen at the lower left of the image.

'BE HEALTHY!'
Soviet-era poster by Liudmila Tarasova depicting a nurse holding newborn twins. The twins and nurse exhort Russians to seek health and well-being.

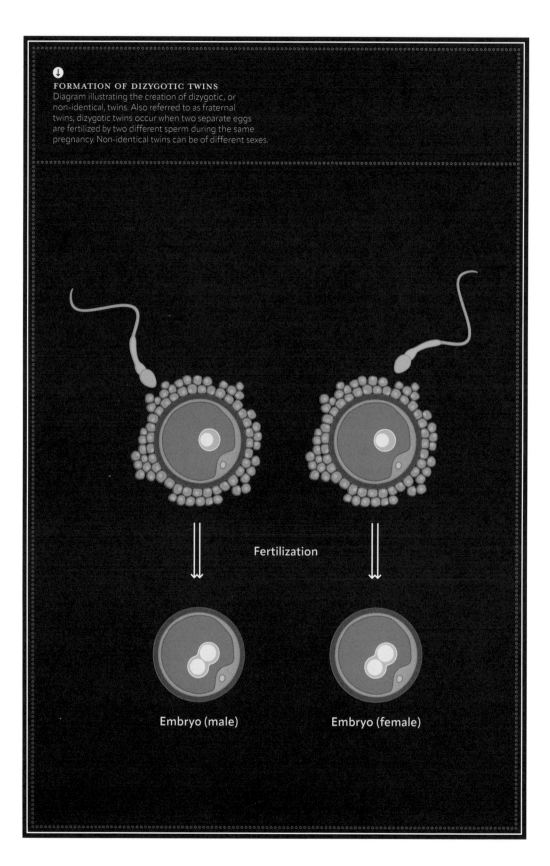

↓

FORMATION OF DIZYGOTIC TWINS
Diagram illustrating the creation of dizygotic, or
non-identical, twins. Also referred to as fraternal
twins, dizygotic twins occur when two separate eggs
are fertilized by two different sperm during the same
pregnancy. Non-identical twins can be of different sexes.

Fertilization

Embryo (male)

Embryo (female)

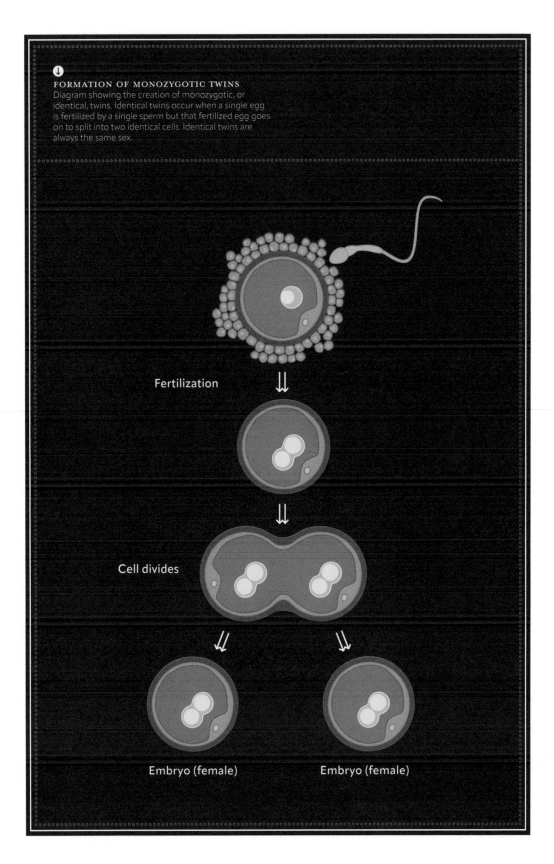

Fertilization

Cell divides

Embryo (female)   Embryo (female)

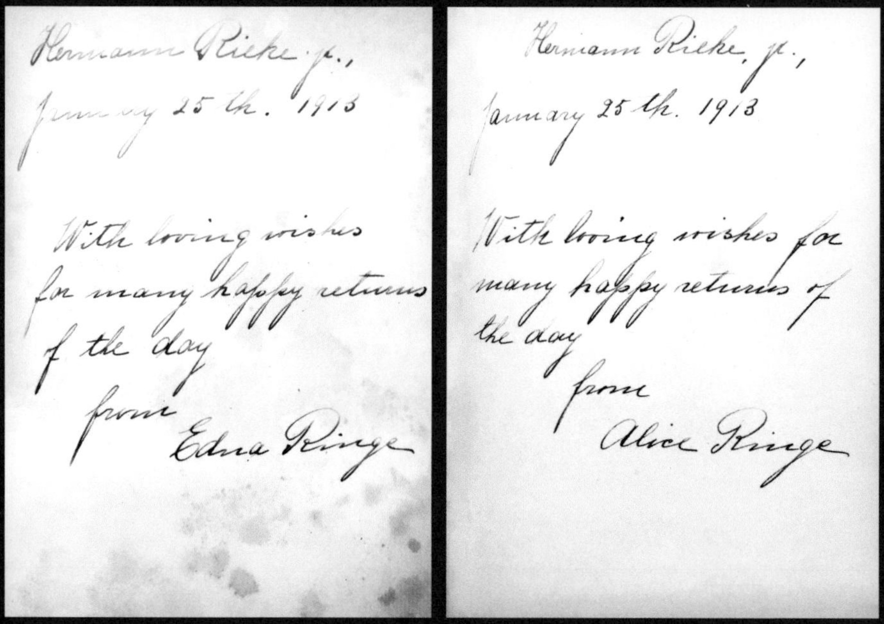
Hermann Rieke, jr.,
January 25 th. 1913
With loving wishes
for many happy returns
of the day
from
Edna Ringe
Hermann Rieke, jr.,
January 25 th. 1913
With loving wishes for
many happy returns of
the day
from
Alice Ringe

1

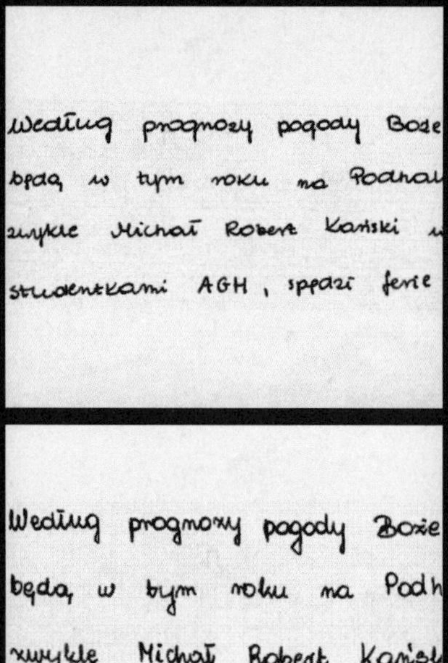
Według prognozy pogody Boże
będą w tym roku na Podhal
zwykle Michał Robert Kański w
studentkami AGH, spędzi ferie
Według prognozy pogody Boże
będą, w tym roku na Podh
zwykle Michał Robert Kańsk
i Dorotą, studentkami AGH

2

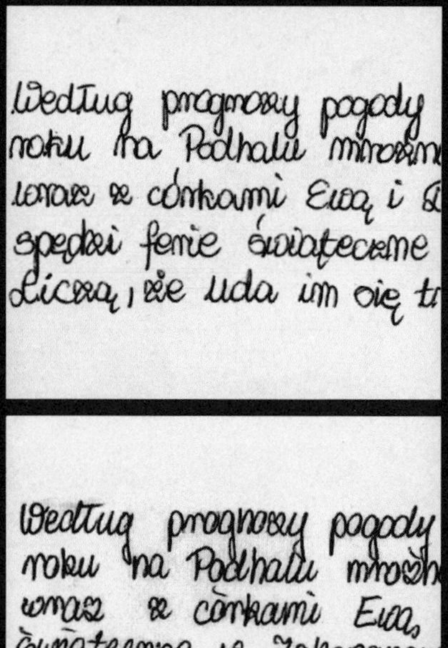
Według prognozy pogody
roku na Podhalu mroźne
wraz ze córkami Ewą i
spędzi ferie świąteczne
Liczą, że uda im się
Według prognozy pogody
roku na Podhalu mroźn
wraz ze córkami Ewą,
świąteczne w Zakopanem
Liczą, że uda im się

3

experimental drama. Appropriately, the phrase has artistic and colonial roots. Shakespeare's play *The Tempest* (*c.* 1610–11) involves Prospero, a magician patriarch who takes command of an enchanted island and its inhabitants, including the enslaved Caliban: 'A devil, a born devil, on whose nature/Nurture can never stick.'

We can think of Galton as a latter-day Prospero, casting a spell and still influencing the lives of twins more than a century later. He demonstrated that twins and twin data can be used experimentally to understand human health and behaviour. In the 1870s Galton's sample was limited to twins who grew up in very similar environments, and among this group he observed them to 'either grow unlike through the development of natural characteristics which had lain dormant at first, or else they continue their lives, keeping time like two watches, hardly to be thrown out of accord except for some physical jar.'[3] With the exception of twins who are raised in different environments, or experience serious illness or injury, Galton concluded that nature prevailed over nurture in the cases he presented.

Since Galton's time, there have been millions of twins measured, tracked, categorized and compared. Twin lives are a means to generate data, to prove and sustain ways of thinking about human life – to produce and explore statistical measures of likelihood and risk. This may make twins feel special or unique. But no twin individual or pair is valuable or useful on its own. They need to be gathered into comparative groups: twin 'types', 'populations' and 'cohorts' that are collective and can be collected as data.

In the 1920s and 1930s, changes in the biological understanding of twins and twinning affected how twins were used. Scientists and doctors identified two types of twins: those born from one fertilized embryo (monozygotic or 'identical' twins) and those born from two or more embryos (dizygotic or 'fraternal' twins). In this early period of human genetics monozygotic twins were labelled genetically identical – assumed to share all their genes. Dizygotic twins were genetically related, like other siblings, and share about 50 per cent of their genes. Since this is not something anyone has control over, scientists call this element in twin studies 'randomization'. Twins will have one or the other genetic relationship with their co-twin. It gives twin studies an objectivity and explanatory power.

One way of using twins involves measuring the frequency of a trait observed in monozygotic twins and comparing it to the frequency observed in dizygotic twins. Scientists realized that they could create a statistical measure of 'heritability', estimating the difference that can be explained by genetic or environmental factors. If monozygotic twins are more alike in height, mathematical ability or eye colour than dizygotic twins, for example, then researchers will conclude that genetics plays a greater role in determining that particular variation. Other experimental designs compare monozygotic twins who are in some way physically or physiologically different – their genetic similarities mean an environmental factor is likely to be revealed. Finally, researchers can look at only monozygotic twins who have grown up in different households. Findings from 'reared-apart' studies can be compared to findings from twins reared together. These

❊ ❊

❶
TWIN HANDWRITING
Birthday wishes written on the same day in 1913 by Edna and Alice, whose identical handwriting led people to believe that they were twins.

❷
DIZYGOTIC HANDWRITING
A comparison of handwriting between non-identical, or fraternal, twins from a 2007 study that used twin handwriting as a phenotype.

❸
MONOZYGOTIC HANDWRITING
A comparison of handwriting between identical twins taken from the same study that used handwriting to express different genetic relationships.

❹
'MENTAL DISORDERS IN TWINS'
Data collected, collated, analysed and presented by psychiatrist and eugenicist Aaron Rosanoff (1878–1943) at the Third International Eugenics Congress, which was held in New York in 1932.

MENTAL DISORDERS IN TWINS

Summary of Material Accumulated to Date (June 1932) in a Study Undertaken by Dr. Aaron J. Rosanoff with the Collaboration of Several Assistants at Los Angeles, California

CLINICAL GROUP	SAME-SEX TWINS PROBABLY MONOZYGOTIC MALES BOTH AFFECTED	ONE AFFECTED	FEMALES BOTH AFFECTED	ONE AFFECTED	PROBABLY DIZYGOTIC MALES BOTH AFFECTED	ONE AFFECTED	FEMALES BOTH AFFECTED	ONE AFFECTED	OPPOSITE-SEX TWINS BOTH AFFECTED	MALE AFFECTED	FEMALE AFFECTED	TOTAL
BEHAVIOR PROBLEMS IN CHILDREN	19	4	18	2	11	10	14	24	7	18	3	130
JUVENILE DELINQUENCY	9	0	4	0	3	1	1	0	2	3	1	24
CRIME (ADULT)	5	1	0	0	1	5	0	0	0	8	0	20
MANIC-DEPRSSIVE PSYCHOSES	4	0	4	0	1	3	0	2	0	2	6	22
DEMENTIA PRAECOX	4	2	6	0	3	2	5	6	2	8	8	46
EPILEPSY	1	1	2	0	0	1	1	1	0	3	3	13
MENTAL DEFICIENCY	38	2	35	5	15	8	18	19	33	31	17	221
MONGOLISM	0	0	1	0	0	0	0	1	0	1	0	3
MISCELLANEOUS	9	3	11	4	4	3	5	9	8	2	5	63
TOTAL	89	13	81	11	38	33	44	62	52	76	43	542

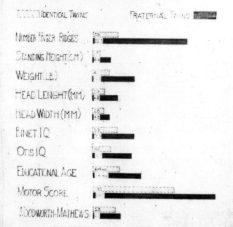

MEAN DIFFERENCES BETWEEN PAIRS OF IDENTICAL AND FRATERNAL TWINS

IDENTICAL TWINS   FRATERNAL TWINS

NUMBER FINGER RIDGES
STANDING HEIGHT (CM)
WEIGHT (LB.)
HEAD LENGHT (MM.)
HEAD WIDTH (MM)
BINET IQ
OTIS IQ
EDUCATIONAL AGE
MOTOR SCORE
WOODWORTH-MATHEWS

INTELLIGENCE AND EDUCATION ACHIEVEMENT OF IDENTICAL TWINS REARED APART

	COMPARATIVE ENVIRONMENT	BINET MENTAL AGE	OTIS MENTAL AGE	EDUCATIONAL AGE
A	POORER			
B	BETTER			
A	POORER			
B	BETTER			
A	SLIGHTLY POORER			
B	SLIGHTLY BETTER			
A	BETTER SOCIAL POSITION			
B	BUT MORE EXACTING			
A	LITTLE DIFFERENCE			
B				
A	SLIGHTLY POORER			
B	SLIGHTLY BETTER			
A	POORER			
B	BETTER			
A	SLIGHTLY POORER			
B	SLIGHTLY BETTER			

STUDIO DEI GEMELLI

The photographs displayed on these two pages are all taken from *Studio dei gemelli* (1951), the work of Italian doctor, geneticist and political activist, Luigi Gedda (1902–2000). He became interested in twins in 1942 after he encountered Romulus and Remus, two physically similar boys. Gedda presented a vast range of published data and studies on twins in one comprehensive volume, adding his own personal commentary throughout.

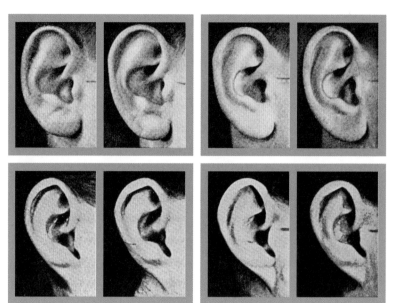

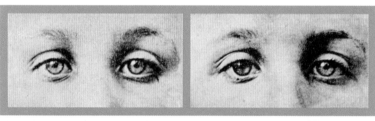

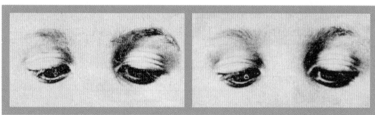

↑

PAIRED EARLOBES

Photographs of the earlobes of two sets of monozygotic twins (with left ears reversed for ease of comparison), taken by Thordar Quelprud in 1932, show a high similarity of appearance.

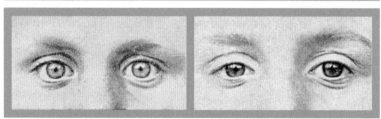

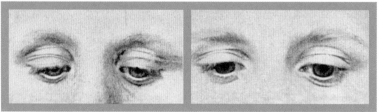

←

PAIRED EYES

Photographs of the eyes of monozygotic twins (top) and dizygotic twins (bottom), both with eyes open and eyes partially closed, taken by Sieder in 1938. The eyes of the monozygotic twins have similar eyebrows, eyelids and eyelashes, while those of the dizygotic twins are more dissimilar.

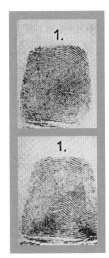

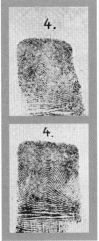
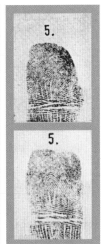

FINGERPRINTS

Right-hand fingerprints of monozygotic twins taken by Reinhold Lotze in 1937 show almost identical characteristics. A significant difference can be seen only in the prints of the fourth fingers. The earlobes of monozygotic twins were observed to vary to a greater degree than those of their fingerprints.

PAIRED IRISES

Photographs of the irises of female monozygotic twins (top) and the irises of male dizygotic twins (bottom) taken by Fritz Schwägerie in 1938. According to Gedda, the irises of the monozygotic twins show almost identical colour and structure, while those of the dizygotic twins show a higher degree of dissimilarity.

TWIN STUDIES

Otmar Freiherr von Verschuer was considered one of the leading twin researchers of his generation, recruiting thousands of twins and establishing large population registers. He trained and collaborated with notorious Nazi-era scientists such as Josef Mengele and Hans Grebe. Verschuer examined sets of twins, ranging from twelve to forty years of age at the Kaiser Wilhelm Institute of Anthropology, Human Heredity and Eugenics between 1942 and 1945, to determine the heritability of medical conditions. Pictured here are twelve-year-old male and sixteen-year-old female twins undergoing anthropometric studies.

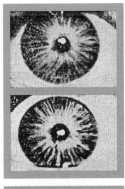
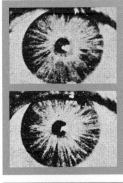
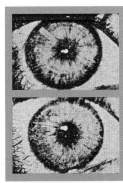
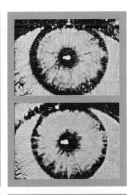
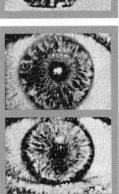
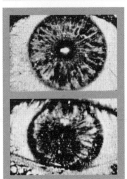
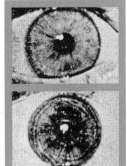
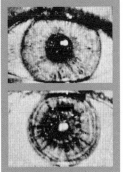

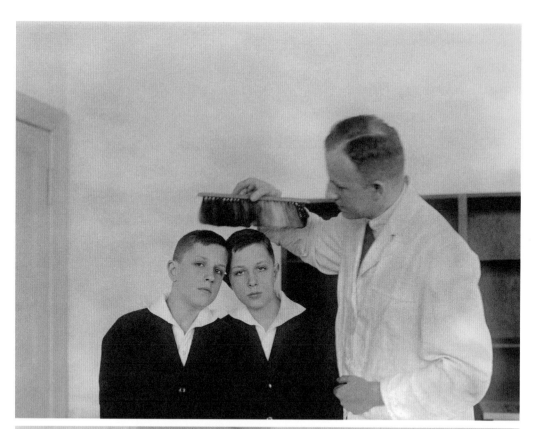

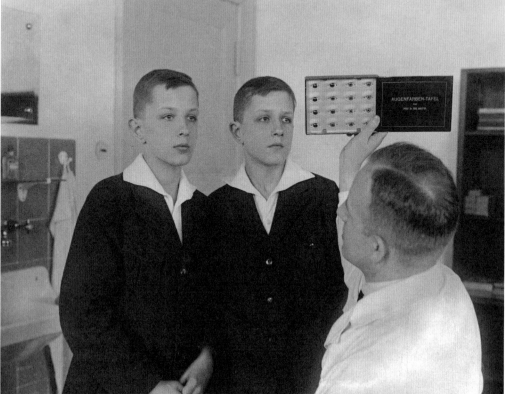

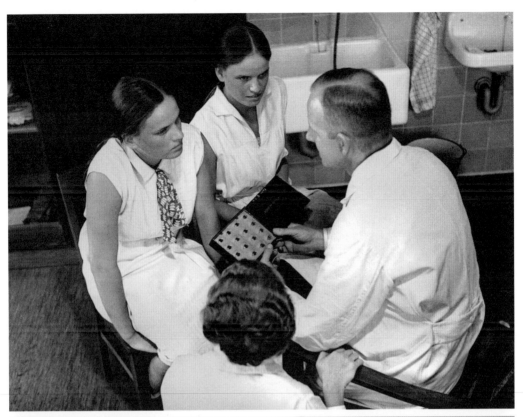

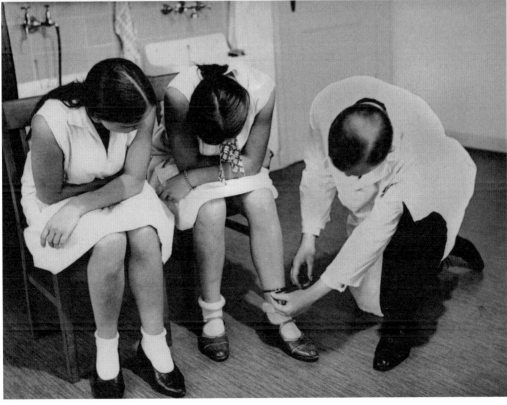

designs are used to understand different contributions made by nature and nurture.

It is hard to understate the impact these studies have had in academic research and beyond. Yet they make fundamental assumptions about what counts as 'genetic', what makes 'an environment' or 'a household'. They also assume that organisms and environments can be usefully separated statistically, and that twins who are born and bred together share their environments, no matter what kind of twin they are. Despite assumptions integral to many twin experiments, these studies promise numerical measures of how much or how little a characteristic can be influenced, shaped or modified. The application of study findings was just as consequential, leading people and groups with 'deficiencies' and 'abnormalities' to be viewed as a risk to themselves, society and nations.

Galton coined the term 'eugenics' in 1883. It means the social and biological improvement of populations based on biometric and psychometric measures of human 'stock'. Eugenics was (and remains) driven by the idea that some socio-economic, national and racial groups have superiority over others. And so politicians, lawyers, medical doctors, artists and writers argued that the quality of populations must be protected and improved. The mentally and physically 'fit' were encouraged to reproduce, while any inferior groups – viewed as physically, mentally and socially 'unfit' – were carefully controlled. The invention of a progressive welfare state – providing mass education, healthcare, housing and criminal justice – is a legacy

of eugenic thinking. So were programmes of mass sterilization and murder. Twins research provided calculations of how much different traits were heritable, and this meant that targeting different groups had a scientific justification.

In 1939, German biologist Otmar Freiherr von Verschuer (1896–1969) addressed the Royal Society in London.[4] He told his audience that Galton had laid the foundations of his current twin research. He and his students were using some of the most widely practised experimental designs, many of which were first developed in Germany. Internationally funded by eugenic foundations such as the Rockefeller and a key figure in the scientific basis of Nazi race laws, Verschuer industrialized the scale of data collection from twins. In the 1930s and 1940s, thousands of twins were recruited to support research at the Institute for Genetic Biology and Racial Hygiene (where he was director from 1935 to 1942), Frankfurt, and then at the Kaiser Wilhelm Institute of Anthropology, Human Heredity, and Eugenics (1942–48), Berlin. He led scientific research into racial typologies. The war allowed closer collaboration with his former students, Josef Mengele (1911–79) and Hans Grebe (1913–99). In 1943, Mengele was appointed doctor at the concentration and extermination camp at Auschwitz-Birkenau, where he conducted experiments on Jewish and Romani twin children, among others. As twins died during these horrific experiments, blood and tissue were sent to Verschuer's laboratories for analysis.[5]

After the war, Verschuer continued his twin research, maintaining prestigious

❈ ❈

 ❶/❷
CSENGERI TWINS
Hungarian twins Lea and Yehudit Csengeri photographed in 1943 after their father was sent to a forced labour camp in Ukraine but before the German occupation of Hungary in March 1944, after which they were deported to Auschwitz with their mother.

❸
AUSCHWITZ CHILD SURVIVORS
Among the child survivors of Auschwitz when it was liberated in 1945 were twins Miriam and Eva Mozes. They are wearing knitted hats to the right of the photograph. They went on to found CANDLES, an education and forgiveness programme.

 ❹
CSENGERI SURVIVAL
In Auschwitz the twins were the subject of medical experiments conducted by Josef Mengele, who wanted to find an objective blood marker for Jewish identity. They survived and returned to Şimleu Silvaniei, where this photograph was taken in 1948.

 ❺
GUTTMANN TWINS
René and Renate Guttmann in Prague, Czechoslovakia, in 1940. In 1943 the twins were sent to Auschwitz. There Josef Mengele separated them, experimenting on Renate and using René as a control. They survived the ordeal, and in 2005 were the subjects of the documentary, *René and I*.

appointments and lecturing to international groups of politically far right and fascist scientists. He cofounded one of the world's leading white supremacist publications, *Mankind Quarterly*, which continues to publish scientific racism. He and his closest collaborators were never fully investigated or they fled without trace. The direct and indirect influence of their work continues into the present, inspiring research in Europe and the United States. Their twin methods encouraged ongoing investigations into the genetic or environmental causes of behaviour, health and disease.

Classical twin designs have been used to produce heritability scores for nail biting, divorce, depression, dog ownership, voting behaviour, criminality and homosexuality, for example – attributing natural or nurtured causes to these behaviours in discrete figures. One common objection to biometrics and psychometrics – the quantification of physiology and health, thought and behaviour – is that they amount to aggregate approximations that are meaningful only for specific groups at particular times. As is common in other areas of biomedical research, twin studies tend to involve older, whiter and wealthier people compared to local and global populations. Consequently, the results of twin research represent just a fraction of the world's genetic and environmental diversity. Despite these shortcomings, findings that claim schizophrenia or intelligence are '70 to 80 per cent heritable' are frequently understood to have universal and predictive value for individuals.[6]

Studies can create great expectations. Having demonstrated that complex behaviours are highly heritable, it was hoped that in the future specific genes might be identified for these behaviours: for example, a gene for epilepsy or general intelligence. Strong counter-arguments came from psychiatrists, psychoanalysts, geneticists and others throughout the 1950s, 1960s and 1970s. They argued that the same methods could be used to demonstrate the importance of the environment in shaping individual and group behaviours. Actual twin people and their lives were caught between different factions in the 'nature vs. nurture' debate. And the consequences of science that claimed schizophrenia or suicide, for example, were more or less due to genetics had implications for all: parents, children, siblings, survivors and victims, both in the past and the future.

In 1979, Jim Lewis knocked on the door of Jim Springer in Dayton, Ohio, and they both learnt they were living a kind of 'double life'. Separated shortly after they were born and reunited at the age of thirty-nine, they came together like lost pieces of a puzzle. They inspected their lives and ran an inventory of affections, afflictions and accomplishments. The twins had been brought up some 65 km (40 miles) apart. Both were called James (or 'Jim' for short) by their adoptive parents. They had both married women called Linda, divorced them, and then remarried women called Betty. One brother named his son James Alan; the other named his son James Allen. They each owned dogs called Toy. They worked various jobs – in security, at petrol stations and at McDonalds – and they took their holidays at the same Florida beach, smoking the same brand of cigarette, sipping the same brand of beer. They bit their nails

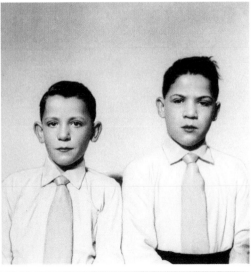
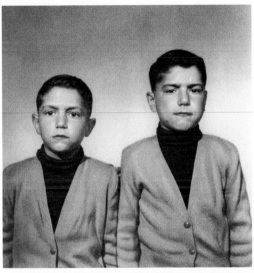
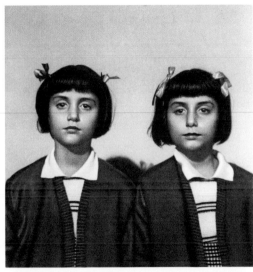
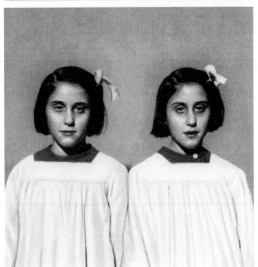
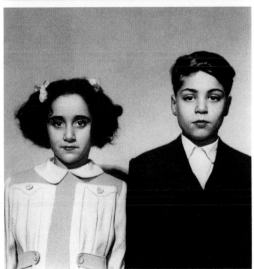

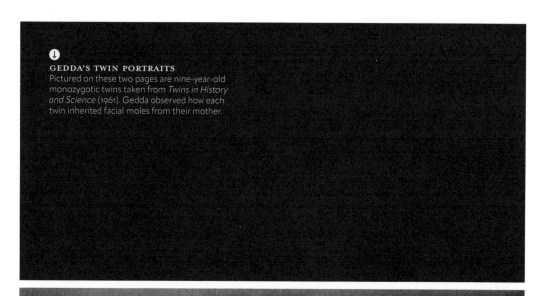

GEDDA'S TWIN PORTRAITS
Pictured on these two pages are nine-year-old
monozygotic twins taken from *Twins in History
and Science* (1961). Gedda observed how each
twin inherited facial moles from their mother.

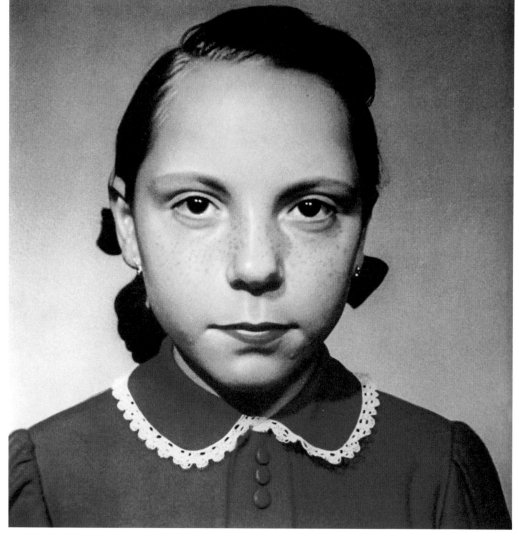

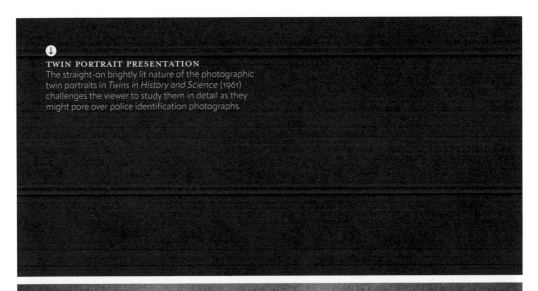

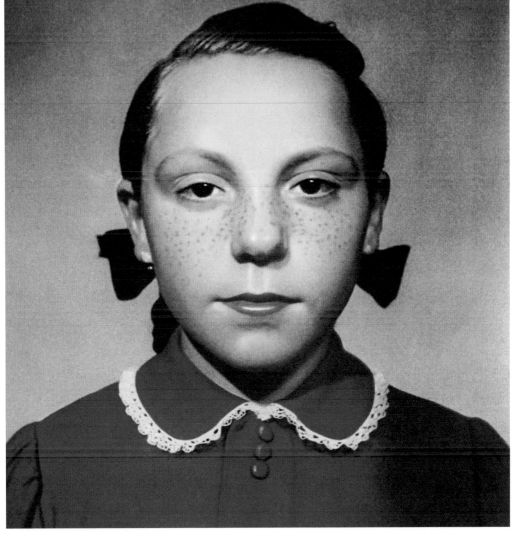

and had been diagnosed with the same chronic health conditions. 'This is really blowing our minds,' Jim Springer told *The New York Times* in 1979. 'Just unbelievable. It's weird. It's downright spooky.'[7]

Pairs of twins separated at birth became key figures in debates about the relative importance of nature and nurture during the 1980s and 1990s. Scientists scrambled for data to support dual hypotheses – natural or social. Either near-identical biology helped the Jim twins name their children James and their dogs Toy, or the brothers lived in a 20th-century US monoculture in which freedom is defined by the products they consumed. The Jim twins were early recruits into MISTRA (Minnesota Study of Twins Reared Apart), and evidence from this study was used to argue that complex human traits were more heritable than previously thought. In general, scientific methods value what can be counted. MISTRA researchers separated biometric and psychometric traits. But there was no overall measure nor explanation for why these idiosyncratic and biographical coincidences piled up in greater numbers between the Jim twins, compared to other twins who had been separated at birth. Over the years, they became iconic, not only for the scientific studies in which they participated but also for how they walked the media circuit.

By the 1980s and 1990s, a resurgent interest in population genetics led to large-scale investment in twin studies. Projects such as MISTRA collected enormous amounts of data on twins separated at or shortly after birth, making measures of their physical and psychological differences when reunited. For a time, these studies made their twin participants media personalities. Television talk show audiences were wowed by these twin marvels. Both scientists and twins benefited from the limelight in different ways. Twins launched media careers, opened twin-themed businesses and enjoyed national celebrity; scientists enjoyed a rare opportunity to communicate their findings to a captive, prime-time audience. Study results, especially those that argued that intelligence is strongly heritable and differently hereditable between racial groups, once more inflamed public debate.

Contemporary twin researchers may be disconcerted by the suggestion that their practices owe much to eugenicist race scientists, fascist war criminals or conspiracists. They prefer to see twin research as a neutral and dispassionate science, free of political history and conducted with the best intentions. Yet, twin methods continue to be used to calculate the relative importance of biological or environmental factors in the sciences of human development, health and disease. And these findings continue to furnish states, corporations, communities and individuals with ways of valuing life – as temporary, unchanging, permanent or plastic, compelled by blind biology or shaped by fortune and misadventure. All of these conclusions have political consequences. They affect how twins and other human groups are respected.

❈ ❈

① LOOK-ALIKE DIZYGOTIC TWINS
Reunited as a result of mistaken identity, the twins became part of the MISTRA study led by Bouchard Jr. and conducted at the University of Minnesota.

② JACK YUFE AND OSKAR STOHR
Identical twins born in 1933, Jack and Oskar were separated at six months. Jack was raised in Trinidad and Oskar in Germany. They joined the MISTRA study in 1980.

③ MOVIE POSTER
The documentary *Three Identical Strangers* (2018) tells the story of triplets Edward Galland, David Kellman and Robert Shafran, adopted by separate parents and reunited at the age of nineteen.

④ JIM LEWIS AND JIM SPRINGER
Separated at four weeks, the Jim twins were reunited at thirty-nine. First to take part in MISTRA in 1979, the media storm helped to recruit many more twins to the study.

⑤ ARO CAMPBELL AND IRIS JOHNS
Separated at six weeks, Aro and Iris met at the age of seventy-five. They spent a week at the MISTRA laboratories answering over 15,000 questions.

Twin and adoptive sibling relations

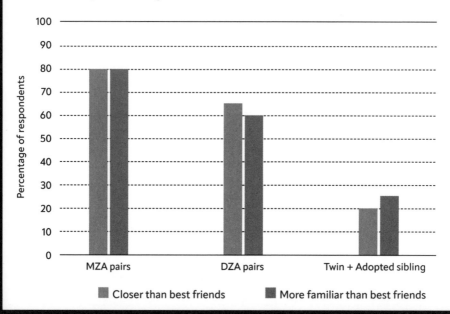

Percentage of respondents

- MZA pairs
- DZA pairs
- Twin + Adopted sibling

■ Closer than best friends   ■ More familiar than best friends

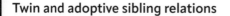

↑ MEASURES OF INTIMACY
Showing differences of familiarity between pairs of identical and fraternal twins reared apart (MZA/DZA) and between a twin and an adopted sibling.

↓ EMOTIONS AND BELIEFS
Showing correlations of complex personality traits in the case of pairs of fraternal and identical twins reared together (DZT/MZT) and MZAs.

Correlations for personality measures

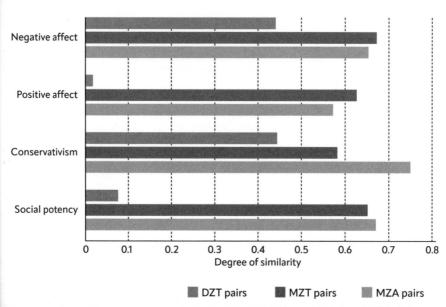

- Negative affect
- Positive affect
- Conservativism
- Social potency

Degree of similarity

■ DZT pairs   ■ MZT pairs   ■ MZA pairs

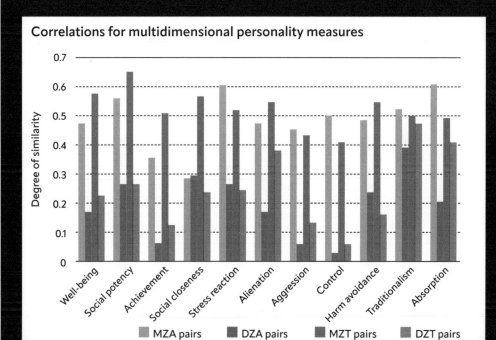

Correlations for multidimensional personality measures

MULTIPLE PERSONALITY TRAITS
Multidimensional tests of personality were used by MISTRA to show degrees of similarity for each trait between twin pairs in each twin category.

GROUP THINK
Showing degrees of similarity of IQ for twin pairs in three twin categories, using Raven and Mill-Hill intelligence tests, plus time spent on each question.

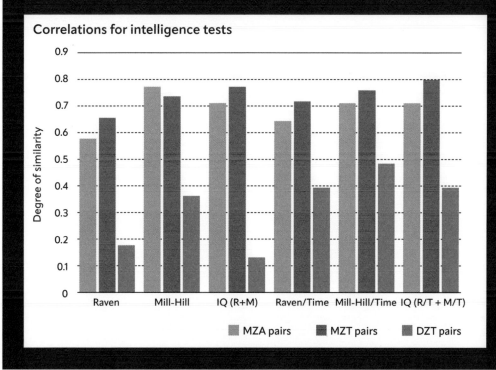

Correlations for intelligence tests

EVA AND JOHANNA
Autistic twin sisters, Eva and Johanna Gill, pictured here at seven years old, posing for a picture at the 32nd annual Twins Day Festival in Twinsburg, Ohio, in 2012.

BEN AND SAM
Ben and Sam Schwenker were diagnosed with autism at eighteen months old. They are pictured here in 2010 when they were six years old, playing together on a trampoline.

For leading twin researchers today, twins offer a rare form of experimental control. For Tim Spector, an eminent twin researcher, they are 'the closest we get to doing animal experiments on humans'.[8] And like animals used in laboratory-based experiments, twins have very little influence on the purpose and direction of the research in which they are involved. 'Twins are rich living laboratories,' says Nancy Segal, another scientist who has studied twins for many years, 'telling us so much about the nuances and vagaries of human behavior just by being themselves.'[9] But who or what is 'telling' remains debated, including by those who use twins in their research.

Twin studies are used to probe the uncertain causes of many disorders and behaviours – including the causes of autism spectrum disorder (ASD) and traits. As in other areas of psychological and psychiatric research, decades of studying twins have guided popular and specialist opinion, affected models of education, care and support, and been used to set further research priorities. Since the late 1970s, findings using classical twin models found high degrees of heritability; there tended to be higher degrees of similarity for ASD among monozygotic twins compared to dizygotic twins. At the time, biological explanations for ASD were welcomed by some parents and caregivers, previously blamed for their 'cold' parenting styles.[10] Comparing estimates from studies contributed to how ASD has been examined from the points of view of age, sex, shared experience and non-shared experience. Far from confirming a binary choice between 'nature and nurture' researchers suggest greater degrees of interaction – 'nature via nurture' or 'nature

of nurture'. This means that twin studies now use categories of nature and nurture that are unrecognizable to the inventors of this science. In recent years, new categories of twin person are also emerging, such that had not been previously thought possible.

Whereas classical twin designs of the 20th century divided twins into two simple groups – monozygotic and dizygotic – powerful sequencing technologies can now decode the whole genomes of twins in less than an hour, and for a few hundred dollars. Since the first human genome (1990–2003) was sequenced, far more is understood about how genes regulate, modify and become inactive over the course of a human life. The field of epigenetics promises to map the many biological interactions between different cells in the human body, such as how and when genes 'express' themselves in a process called DNA methylation.[11] By mapping the molecules around the genome, scientists have been eager to show how monozygotic twin pairs are genetically different in terms of biological action and function; before and after birth, the molecular identities of twins evolve.

One study, involving 381 monozygotic twin pairs and their immediate family members, concluded that as much as 15 per cent of monozygotic twins have many different mutations that are not shared by their brother or sister.[12] The group hypothesized that it was possible that the sequenced mutations in monozygotic twins occur either at the point of becoming twins or *because* they are twins. Kári Stefánsson, the scientist leading the research, explained that although we think of monozygotic twins

as equals, their differences go back to the undifferentiated ball of cells in the embryo:

> We have found a twin pair where one of the twins has mutations in all cells of his body, and they are not found in any cell in the body of the other twin ... we have found twins when the mutation is found in all cells in the body of one of the twins, and in 20 percent of the cells in the body of the other twin ... it looks like coincidence is an extraordinarily important factor in which cells in the inner cell mass go into making a person.[13]

Stefánsson concluded: 'We have to be very careful when we are using twins as a model.' In the future, scientists may seek to put twins into ever-more refined groups of people based on shared degrees of difference.

Another study of twin DNA methylation data, conducted in 2021, found that a number of biomarkers were stable from birth through to adulthood. In essence, molecular mutations could identify monozygotic twins, without matching them to the data of their co-twins. Twins carry unique markers because they are conceived as twins. This technique provides hope for scientists who want to unravel the mechanisms that cause a zygote to split. But scientists also hope to resolve all kinds of other mysteries: the technique provides laboratory proof that what becomes a single life may start as two. It may help to resolve instances of child theft, separation and adoption, or it may even establish the twinship of historical figures. And it serves as the first stage in people's search for lost siblings.

Comparisons based on cases were shaped by 19th-century ideas of individuals nested in statistical populations. The same ideas convinced scientists that twins could be used as tools of discovery, or a way of weighing nature and nurture on a set of scales. Now, a combination of fine-grained biochemistry and powerful computational processing has led to key assumptions about twins and singletons to be questioned. The qualities and kinds of twin individuals, and the sorting methods used to build populations, have come under renewed scrutiny.

Both the sciences and the arts confront what it means to be visually, biologically and genealogically related. Since 2000, Canadian artist François Brunelle (b. 1950) has photographed look-alike pairs around the globe: unknown twins, stranger twins, doubles and doppelgängers. They are people who look alike, but may never have met. In an era of social media, these matches occur globally, meeting together in Brunelle's studio.

In 2022, a team of Spanish researchers recruited a small number of unrelated look-alike pairs.[14] They scanned the photographic images of their faces and compared their genomes, methylation signatures and microbes. They found that while their faces showed very high levels of anthropometric similarity and their genomes were moderately similar, their methylation and microbial profiles were very different. Unrelated look-alikes could, therefore, prove increasingly useful for identifying different kinds of molecular relations between people. This is twin science turned inside out. It might reopen the nature vs. nurture debate along renewed lines of enquiry. With each reopening, twins and their avatars are both witnesses and sources of evidence. ✿✿

❋❋ ... your strange, ludicrous ... impossible desire to seem to be my twin, and to pass yourself off as such will only lead to ... defeat. ❋❋

Fyodor Dostoevsky, *The Double*, 1846

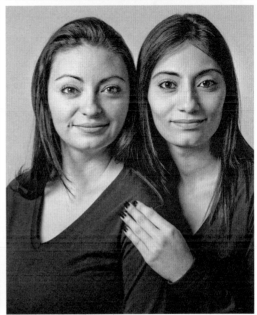

SCOTT AND MARK KELLY
In 2015 the twins participated in NASA's Twin Study. Scott spent a year in space and his brother, also an astronaut, remained on Earth as a control. The study applied the traditions of twin studies with the latest sequencing technologies. The aim was to understand the biological effects of space travel.

THE T**WINS** STUDY

CSU JHU NASA NU SU UCSD UPenn WCMC wyle

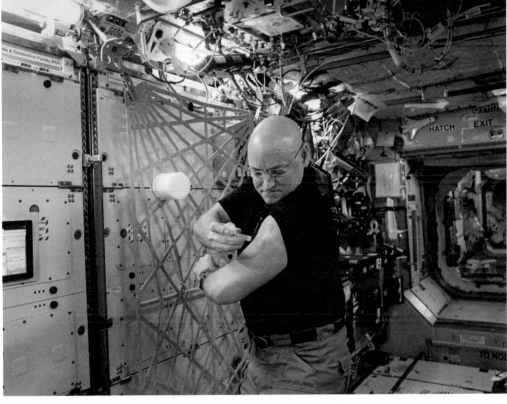

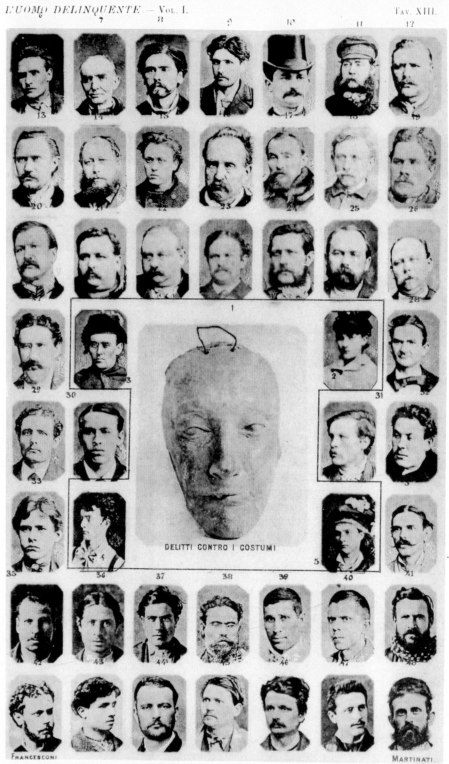

DELITTI CONTRO I COSTUMI

FRANCESCONI

MARTINATI

RITRATTI DI CRIMINALI TEDESCHI ED ITALIANI.

v. Crime *and* Forensics

✵ ✵

In 2008, highway police stopped Swedish twins Sabina and Ursula Eriksson walking down the central reservation of Britain's busiest motorway.[1] The police arrived with a film crew expecting a routine call, and at first the twins seemed calm and spoke to officers by the side of the road. But then Ursula leapt into the path of a truck travelling at more than 80 kph (50 mph). Her legs were crushed by the impact. Her twin sister followed her into the road, crashing into a car that knocked her unconscious. Ursula was taken to hospital. Sabina was taken to a local police station, where she was charged with trespassing and assaulting a police officer. Here, Sabina told a policeman: 'We say in Sweden that an accident rarely comes alone. Usually at least one more follows – maybe two.'[2]

The following day, as her sister recovered in hospital, Sabina left the police station. She met two men to whom she spoke about finding accommodation for the night. She befriended them and was invited to stay with Glenn Hollinshead. The next day, for reasons never fully understood, Sabina stabbed Hollinshead to death. She went on the run and was seen by witnesses hitting herself over the head with a hammer before jumping 12 m (40 ft) down onto the A50, another busy road, breaking her legs and fracturing her skull.[3]

Following a trial, Sabina was imprisoned for five years. In the courtroom, her barrister argued for her diminished responsibility, emphasizing the role of twinship itself as the underlying cause of a shared psychosis. The twins were 'living in their own world,' he said, 'they had an enormously strong bond as twins. At some stage the defendant's own psyche was overborne by her sister's illness.' The twins experienced a rare psychiatric condition known colloquially as *folie à deux* (madness of two), or by its medical term 'shared psychotic disorder'. Sabina's barrister claimed she was a secondary sufferer, meaning that Ursula's delusions triggered the onset of Sabina's symptoms. There is no agreed definition of shared psychotic disorder or how a strong bond with a twin or anyone else can be its trigger.

Criminal cases are built on an individualized idea of choice and motivation, definitions most routinely attributed to one legal person. The idea that twins are rule breakers is common in screen and literary representations. They are portrayed as 'double trouble' conspirators who trespass on biological and social conventions. As a consequence, there remains a generous cultural space given to real twins who live a life of misrule.

Reginald and Ronald Kray are another example of how lives of crime and twin lives become inseparable, suggesting to some that there may be a causal link. Growing up in London's East End, the Krays ended their National Service with dishonourable discharge. They became notoriously violent organized criminals. Beginning with robbery, extortion and money laundering, and then murder, they later owned West London nightclubs and enjoyed the company of film stars, politicians, artists and musicians. They

←

PORTRAITS OF GERMAN AND ITALIAN CRIMINALS
Taken from *L'uomo delinquente* (1889) by Cesare Lombroso (1835–1909), who believed that criminals could be identified by certain physical characteristics and that their behaviour was inherited.

PHYSIOGNOMY OF EVIL CHARACTERISTICS

Johann Kaspar Lavater (1741–1801) held that physiognomy related to character traits of individuals. These images, taken from *Nouveau Lavater Complet* (1842), illustrate Lavater's criminal facial types and draw attention to the resemblance of each type to different animal species.

THE DELINQUENT MAN
Lombroso classified individuals into types according to physical characteristics. He believed that criminal types could be identified by such characteristics as a sloping forehead, asymmetric face or large ears, and that their criminal behaviours were inherited with those traits.

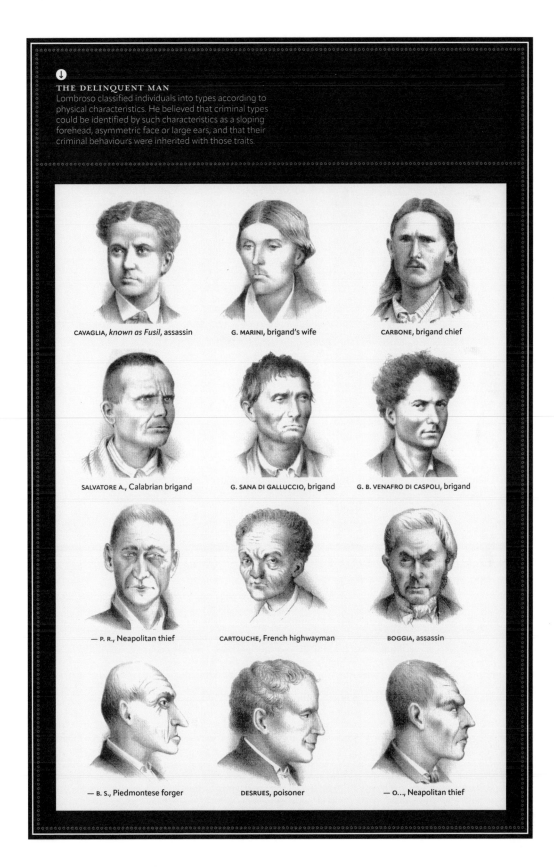

CAVAGLIA, *known as Fusil*, assassin

G. MARINI, brigand's wife

CARBONE, brigand chief

SALVATORE A., Calabrian brigand

G. SANA DI GALLUCCIO, brigand

G. B. VENAFRO DI CASPOLI, brigand

— P. R., Neapolitan thief

CARTOUCHE, French highwayman

BOGGIA, assassin

— B. S., Piedmontese forger

DESRUES, poisoner

— O..., Neapolitan thief

❋❋Although they were obviously identical twins, Reggie was very different – thinner, quicker, with a certain shifty charm. ❋❋

John Pearson, *The Profession of Violence: The Rise and Fall of the Kray Twins*, 1972

THE KRAY TWINS
Ronald and Reginald Kray, pictured here aged twenty, boxed professionally. Ronnie fought six times, winning four fights by knockout and losing two by decision. Reggie was unbeaten, winning all seven of his professional fights.

were unusual for wanting fame while also terrorizing people. Finally, they were arrested and given life sentences in 1969. They spent the rest of their lives in different prisons. Ronnie's diagnosis of violent schizophrenia placed him in Broadmoor, one of England's highest-security prisons. He died there aged sixty-one. Reggie was given early release on compassionate grounds and he died days later, aged sixty-six. As his coffin was brought to rest with his brother's remains, thousands of cheering fans lined the streets. The twins' reputation was crafted over half a lifetime behind bars, embroidered by biographies, television and newspaper interviews, films and documentaries. Ronnie said in his autobiography: '... me and my brother ruled London. We were fucking untouchable ....'[4] At the time of writing this, he had been in prison for more than twenty years – the objective was to maintain an unassailable reputation. It is still possible to walk into an East End pub and meet men willing to recount rose-tinted stories about the Krays. Others are less keen to share their trauma.

As glamour gangsters, the Krays courted the limelight, trading on the fascination that people have for twins. Ronnie was openly gay. And after he was imprisoned, Reggie explained that he was bisexual. Rumours about their sexuality, including sexual relations they may have had with each other, joined other speculations about how their twin relations shaped their criminal successes and failures.[5] Ronnie's diagnosis of paranoid schizophrenia fuels common links made between violence and mental illness, yet Reg had no such diagnosis. Their notoriety was enhanced by an explosive inscrutability that

appears easily conflated with the condition of being a twin – glamorized and sensationalized, the consequences of violence glossed over. 'Ronnie and Reggie' – a double act viewed by the light of a nostalgic glitter ball.

Twin crime is explained by changing expectations about twins. But twins are also used to test a hypothesis that affects comparisons between twins and everyone else: are we all capable of crime? Are some people more likely to commit crimes than others? Since the 1930s, scientists have used classical twin study designs to measure if people are born to be bad. They compare crime rates between monozygotic and dizygotic twins to estimate the genetic and social contributions of antisocial behaviour, delinquency and criminal convictions.[6] These studies found greater rates of concordance between monozygotic twins, and concluded that a substantial amount of the variation in crime-related behaviours is explained by genetic factors – between 30 and 90 per cent in some studies. Accordingly, shared environmental factors are reported to play a negligible role. This does important things for how and when we think criminality occurs, and impacts the policies recommended to curb behaviour and seek reform in individuals.

Twins have been defining the limits of the law for many years. Twin studies may not make them uniquely criminal as a group, but they do make twins the experimental workhorses for a biological understanding of crime. Although the results speak for populations and are not predictive for individuals, they focus attention on the biological causes of crime rather than what friends, families and communities may do to prevent it. As critics

REGGIE AND SHIRLEY BASSEY
The twins cultivated celebrity and glamour.
Here, Reggie Kray (third from right) can be seen
with singer Shirley Bassey in a nightclub in 1965.

THE KRAYS AND JUDY GARLAND
American actress and singer Judy Garland,
with her husband Mark Herron (left), visit
Ronnie and Reggie Kray in 1964.

⇑ THE KRAYS AND BARBARA WINDSOR
Pictured here (left to right) are actor George
Sewell, Reggie Kray, actress Barbara Windsor and
Ronnie Kray at the El Morocco nightclub in 1965.

↑ RONNIE WITH CHRISTINE KEELER
Ronnie Kray sits to the left of Christine Keeler in
a nightclub in 1969. Her high-profile affair with war
minister John Profumo had made her a celebrity.

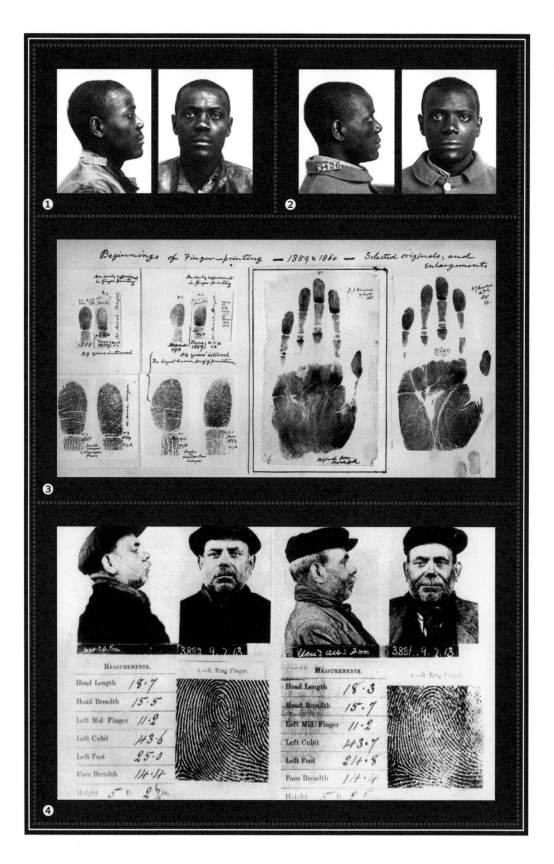

of twin studies point out, breaking the law and prosecuting a crime are not the same thing.

Some of the key ingredients of modern criminal investigation involve data collection, retrieval and management. French researcher Alphonse Bertillon (1853–1914) introduced his 'Bertillon system' or 'Bertillonage' in the 1880s. It is now considered the world's first universal standardized criminal database. These records included various measurements of the head, limbs and feet, and a photographic headshot taken from the front and side: an early 'mug shot' that is still a key part of contemporary criminal records. Bertillon believed that one day every person may have such a record, amounting to a centralized surveillance database.

Subsequently, twins have been used to expose flaws in Bertillon's records and have influenced the creation of alternative systems of identification. Extraordinary instances of confused identity were used to make the case for other methods, particularly forensic fingerprinting. In May 1903, Will West was sent to prison. On arrival at US Penitentiary Leavenworth, Kansas, prison staff completed his Bertillon record and were dismayed to find his measurements were identical to those of an existing inmate, one William West, who was serving a life sentence. Their photographs appeared to be identical. 'That's my picture,' confirmed Will West, 'but I don't know where you got it, for I know I have never been here before.' Identical in name, image and in other physical features, the key to the Wests' differences lay at the tips of their fingers.[7]

The transition from Bertillon's system to forensic fingerprinting involved Bertillon and Francis Galton classifying hundreds of prisoner fingerprints as part of a systematic investigation.[8] Some of these techniques were applied in colonial India by Edward Henry (1850–1931), who returned to London in 1901 to take up the position of Assistant Commissioner (Crime). He established the Metropolitan Police Fingerprint Bureau, where he instituted forensic fingerprinting and the Henry system. Not unlike Galton, who turned to twins to create comparative groups, Henry needed to prove that it was impossible for two people to share the same fingerprint. He did so by scouring England's prisons for twins. He met Ebenezer Albert and Albert Ebenezer Fox, known as the 'Twin Foxes', who were notorious poachers with hundreds of convictions between them. According to a profile in *The New York Times*, the Twin Foxes shared an extraordinary physical resemblance – so remarkable that it led to wrongful prosecution:

> ... owing to the stupidity of gamekeepers and police, the non-offending brother has suffered conviction in almost every other instance. For years they have borne these mistakes in silence. But now the soul of each burns at the thought of the injustice done to his brother.[9]

The Twin Foxes participated in Henry's research and, as prolific thieves, were among the first people to be convicted using fingerprinting technology.[10] So, it is true that even monozygotic twins have different fingerprints. We know this because before scientists established monozygotic and dizygotic twin categories in the 1920s and 1930s, twins were key to establishing fingerprinting as part of routine police investigation.

Anthropometry, fingerprinting, DNA testing and, more recently, artificial intelligence (AI) can be used to advance 19th-century interests in testing and comparing individuals, and

❶ WILLIAM WEST MUG SHOT
William West was serving a life sentence at US Penitentiary Leavenworth when his twin, Will West, arrived in 1903. Their Bertillon records matched.

❷ WILL WEST MUG SHOT
Will West's photograph appeared identical to his brother's. In 1905, after the fingerprint system had been installed, their fingerprints were taken and compared.

❸ FINGERPRINTS TAKEN BY HERSCHEL

Experiments conducted by William Herschel (1833–1917), showing his and others' prints, taken while at the Indian civil service (c. 1859–1913).

❹ THE FOX TWINS

Master poachers Albert Ebenezer and Ebenezer Albert Fox were measured and fingerprinted by the expanded Bertillon system, which was in use by 1913.

⊝ **TRAINING IN THE BERTILLON SYSTEM**
Bertillon's class on the spoken portrait (or *portrait parlé*), 1911, stressed the importance of photography and body measurements to create a precise record of identifiers that could be used to track suspects.

⊙ **ANTHROPOMETRIC IDENTIFICATION I**
Unrelated individuals are shown to share a physical resemblance in these pages taken from Bertillon's *Identification anthropométrique: Instructions signalétiques* (1893).

●
ANTHROPOMETRIC IDENTIFICATION II
Photographs of four sets of people revealing how
their physical appearance changed over different
periods of time, taken from Bertillon's *Identification
anthropométrique: Instructions signalétiques* (1893).

sorting them into populations. Individuals and populations evolve together in meaning and scale. At each stage of development, however, twins and twin criminals have marked the quantitative sensitivity and accuracy of technological systems, their underlying logic of part and whole, likeness and difference, individual and population.

There is a special notoriety reserved for look-alike twins who escape or evade the law. And this is even greater for those twins who seem to expose the unjust fragility and arbitrariness of legal systems. In the early 1950s Charles and George Finn wanted to set up The Flying Finn Twins Airline Inc. They bought a decommissioned military transport plane. Unfortunately, the US federal government argued that the Finns had no right to buy a plane of this kind. The litigants stood their ground. Arrests followed legal battles. The twins made a street-level citizen's arrest of the US attorney leading the prosecution. And then the twins took flight – stealing their plane and hiding it in Nevada. Grand Jury indictments collapsed when witnesses in this case were unable to identify which Finn twin was responsible. The press, of course, loved them.

Forensic DNA testing was introduced as evidence in US courtrooms in the 1980s and became common by the mid-1990s. Like all evidence used to prosecute criminals, DNA profiling was first opposed on a technical basis. Critics pointed to how techniques lacked accuracy. Laboratory methods needed to be standardized for courtrooms to be less hostile towards the technology as a whole. But in a relatively short period of time DNA data grew into a necessary tool for

justice, just as a telescope is felt necessary for mapping the stars.

It was in the period just before the widespread use of forensic DNA that Pat and Pete Bondurant murdered Gwen Dugger, Ronnie Gaines and Terry Lynn Clark near Pulaski, Tennessee, USA. Each wearing flannel shirts, and weighing 150 kg (c. 350 lb), they built fearsome reputations among local communities as violent eccentrics. It was only after Pat's estranged wife Denise Bondurant testified against them that the police were able to build enough evidence to convict them for murder.

As DNA's reputation became synonymous with cast-iron proof, cases arose that tested DNA forensics and its power to mark individual suspects. Many of these involved twins. In 1999, a young woman was raped in Grand Rapids, Michigan. It took five years for the police to match DNA evidence to a man called Jerome Cooper. And yet Jerome had a twin brother, Tyrone, whose DNA was also a match. There was no other evidence available, no witnesses. Both twins had previous convictions for sexual assault. Both also denied involvement in the case. Neither was prepared to conclude the case and provide further evidence of the other's guilt or innocence. More than twenty years later, this cold case is kept warm by changes in DNA sequencing. News reporters and science correspondents return to it routinely, as a narrative foil for a technological quick fix for the US criminal justice system. The evasion of justice by some twin people brings the limelight to twins themselves, as legal trickster figures. Very rarely do they acknowledge the position of victims,

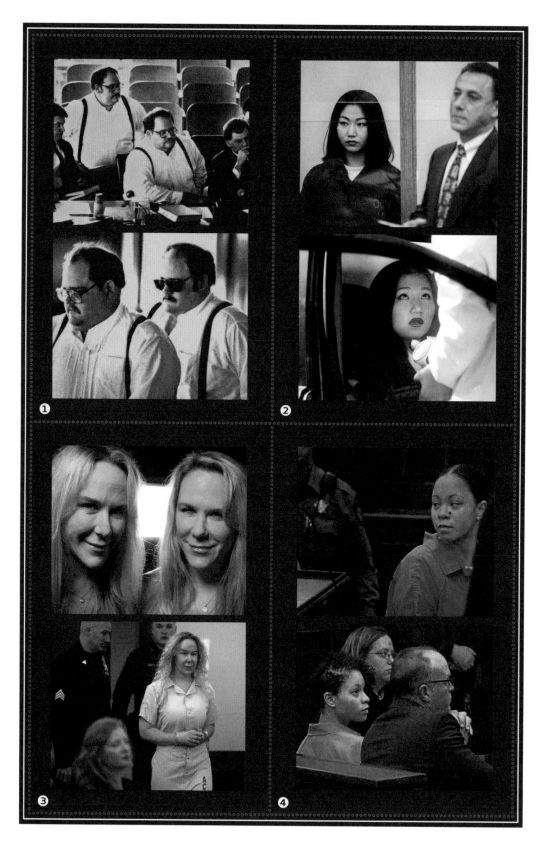

the politics of policing or the causes of sexual assault.

If one of the powers granted to genetic forensics is the ability to identify individuals, then the legal system's inability to discriminate between some twins creates bizarre and paradoxical outcomes. In 2009, Abbas and Hassan O (their names are protected under German law) stole jewelry valued at €5 million from Berlin's well-known department store Kaufhaus des Westens (KaDeWe). The twins were identified on CCTV, and a glove left at the crime scene contained DNA traces that matched both brothers. Neither could be convicted.[11] Twins who dodge the system expose a forensic weakness, that in almost all other cases is a forensic strength.

Forensic geneticists have known that twins are not genetically identical for many years. They point to whole genome and whole exome sequencing rather than the more selective, faster and cheaper methods that are currently standard. As with Bertillon, technology needs to be widely used. The same applies for controversial automatic facial recognition systems. Facial recognition is used for border and national security, as well as for access to some social welfare and other government programmes. It is also a key component of web services, home security and other consumer goods. These, too, must be trained on a wide variety of people. Computer scientists developing these algorithms struggle with twins who are very visually alike, and so algorithms misrecognize individuals.

Consumer electronics that use simple facial ID for access can fail the 'twin test' of two people who look alike. Humans, however, tend to outperform recognition technologies when sorting twin from twin. This balance between human and computer capacity is gradually changing.[12] Studies have found that algorithmic tests can accurately discriminate between twins, as long as images are taken in controlled conditions. In general, machine-learning algorithms are built up from groups of images, learning differences between individuals rather than coding images according to their similarities. This means they have an in-built, twin-shaped bias towards people who are visually alike. One solution sorts images based on likeness, producing finer pairings based on a learning process. From thousands of images, identical twins are scored for likeness. These pairs become a statistical baseline used to rank all the other images of twins and non-twins according to an in-group scale of likeness.

The history of forensic science is a history of standardized pattern recognition. Twins are frequently outliers because they are disruptive to biometric standards that contrast individuals with populations. This brought celebrity and notoriety to some twin people who committed crimes and evaded prosecution. Experimental statistical parameters of visual and biometric likeness are another legacy of an applied science of twins and twinning. Attempts to build machine-learning algorithms using twins extends a long-standing role for twins to test and be tested on. ✸✸

 THE BONDURANT TWINS
Pat and Pete Bondurant appear in court in 1991. Known as the 'Killer Siblings', they were convicted of the murders of three individuals in the 1980s.

 THE HAN TWINS
Jeena and Sunny Han appear at the 'Orange County Evil Twin Trial' in 1997. Jeena (top) was accused of plotting to murder her twin sister Sunny (below).

 THE DUVAL TWINS
Alexandria and Anastasia Duval in 2008 (top) and Alexandria (below) in court in 2016, where she was tried for murdering her sister; she was acquitted.

 THE WHITEHEAD TWINS
Jasmiyah (top) and Tasmiyah Whitehead in court in 2014 for the killing of their mother Jarmecca in 2010. They pleaded guilty to manslaughter.

VI. Born *and* Made

⁕ ⁕

One of Hollywood's best-loved films about twins features Arnold Schwarzenegger (b. 1947) and Danny DeVito (b. 1944) playing estranged brothers Julius and Vincent Benedict. Released in 1988, *Twins* cast Schwarzenegger in his first comedic role as a colossal action hero delivering one-liners with muscle. In the film, the twins grow up without knowing each other. Julius (Schwarzenegger) lives on a luxurious Pacific island, absorbed in learning. At the age of thirty-five, he discovers he has a twin and goes looking for his brother in Los Angeles. There, he finds the streetwise Vincent (DeVito), raised in an orphanage, who struggles to believe he is a twin to this superman.

The film aims to laugh at Western beliefs about who should be twins. Core to its comedy is the seemingly absurd yet entirely plausible idea that an Austrian-born bodybuilder could be the twin of a disabled US actor affected by a rare genetic disorder.[1] The rest is satire: Julius and Vincent are a bungled outcome of an experiment that aimed to make the perfect child using the DNA of six fathers and one mother. Their separation into extremes of wealth and poverty and their eventual reunification respond to sensational reared-apart studies that captured the interests of

US audiences throughout the 1980s. The making and success of *Twins* combined the drama of twin separation and reunion with fears attached to eugenics and gene editing.

Whether or not *Twins* makes you laugh or despair, it documents an important cultural change in human society. Over the centuries, the creation of twins has attracted different explanations and reactions. Twin people have been valued by different people at different times for very different reasons. Only in the early 1980s, in some wealthy and industrialized countries, did it become possible to purposefully create twins. In Australia in 1981, Stephen and Amanda Mays were the first twins born via *in vitro* fertilization (IVF). In the decades that followed, millions more would be born using similar techniques.

For most of the 20th century, twins have been born at a relatively steady rate. In the United States, for example, from the 1910s to the 1980s, twins made up about 2 per cent of all recorded births each year. From the early 1980s, the number of twins born each year began to increase. In 1980, one in every 53 births was a twin. By 2014, this had increased to one in every 29 births: an overall increase of 73 per cent.[2] Commentators have called this a 'twin epidemic' and a 'multiple birth explosion'.[3]

Assisted reproduction technologies (ART) come in many different forms. This is one reason why they make different kinds of twin, adding new types and categories to those already familiar to us. In the mid-1980s, it became possible to use hormones to induce multi-ovulation. One clinician interviewed in 1995 described the liberal use of these drugs in private US fertility clinics: '... [it is] as if they were prescribing bubble gum at

IN VITRO FERTILIZATION
Computer illustration showing an egg that has been removed from the ovary being injected with sperm in a laboratory before being implanted back into the uterus.

***TWINS* MOVIE POSTERS**
Arnold Schwarzenegger and Danny DeVito are cast as unlikely twins in the 1988 movie *Twins*. On the posters their names are reversed, reinforcing the absurdity of the two being confused, which is played out in the film.

DEVITO

SCHWARZENEGGER

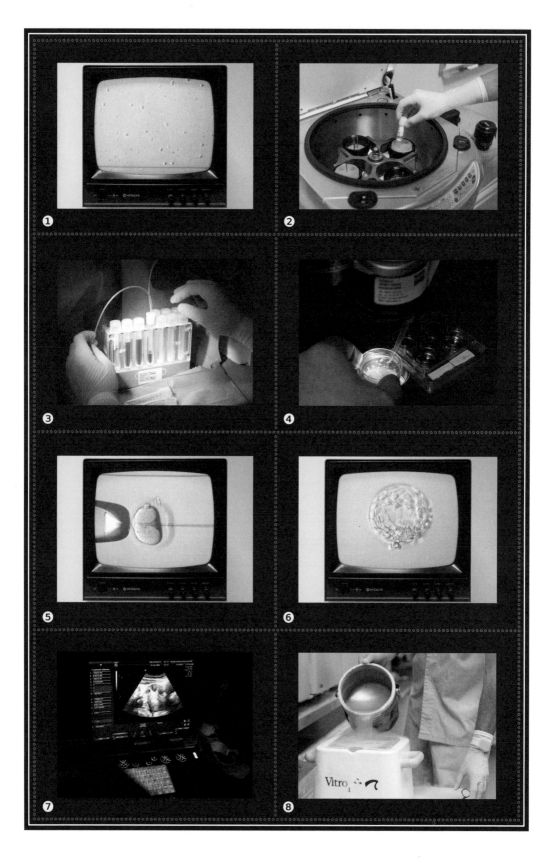

a children's birthday party'.[4] Hormones can stimulate ovaries into releasing many eggs in a menstrual cycle, thereby increasing the likelihood of conceiving twins.

IVF involves the extraction of many eggs, after which they can be fertilized with sperm *in vitro*. Fertilized embryos are then transferred so that they can develop *in utero*. To increase the chances of conception, it became common practice for more than one embryo to be transferred in a cycle of IVF. This led to the creation of many twin and higher order multiples. These technologies tend to increase the likelihood of creating dizygotic twins, because different eggs will be fertilized by different sperm before being implanted. But the manipulation of embryos in laboratory environments increases rates of monozygotic splitting, too. Even single-embryo transfers can result in the splitting of zygotes and thus increase rates of twin pregnancy.[5]

Trade in donated sperm and eggs means that twins can be born to parents who are not their biological or legal relation. Some interventions create twins with no genetic relationship to each other, using eggs and sperm from different donors. In this sense, technology and contract law bend older cultural definitions of twins and twinning; these once assumed that twins are, by definition, those people conceived, born and raised together. While IVF-conceived twins can be born together, they might also have different biological mothers and fathers and legal parents. They can be born via surrogate mothers to whom a biological relationship is qualified by law.

The ability to cryogenically freeze embryos means that the birth of 'twiblings' can occur through different pregnancies – conceived together but born apart.[6] US anthropologist Sarah Franklin (b. 1960) has called this 'biological relativity' – an evolving combination of technology, biology and social kinship ties.[7] Bioscience is adapting kinship relations at a molecular level, while what we think of as biologically 'natural' has also undergone manipulation.

As a desirable, remarkable, exceptional kind of people, twins are historically connected to the genealogies of the superhuman and supernatural, and they are selected to accompany political efforts to reform families and family values. For minoritized groups, the birth of twins can signal a progressive break from heterosexual conventions. Lesbians and trans men can use donor sperm and conceive via IVF or other means. They may opt for reciprocal IVF, where one partner uses their eggs – retrieved and fertilized using donated sperm in IVF – and the resulting embryos are then implanted into the other partner for pregnancy. Reciprocity can be doubled, so that both carry foetuses in tandem. Gay men have also sought twins as a way of 'completing' a family that can revise gender and sexual dynamics of reproduction and family. The first gay men in Britain to use IVF conceived twins via a gestational surrogate. Each twin had the same biological mother, different biological fathers and the same legal parents.

IVF and other assisted fertility treatments have allowed millions of parents to welcome

---

❋ ❋

❶ SPERM MOBILITY
At the assisted reproductive technology (ART) laboratory, sperm are studied for their mobility.

❷ CENTRIFUGATION
Mature normal sperm are separated from immature abnormal sperm by density gradient centrifugation.

❸ FOLLICLE PUNCTURE
In the operating theatre, a follicle in the ovary is punctured and the oocytes (immature egg cells) are extracted.

❹ PREPARING OOCYTES
In the laboratory cumulus cells are removed from the oocytes to prepare them to receive the sperm.

❺ SPERM INJECTION
The prepared sperm are injected directly into each oocyte using a micropipette. Fertilization takes c. 18 hours.

❻ EMBRYO CULTURE
After 2–4 days blastocyst culture (embryos grown in the laboratory) is graded for development and quality.

❼ TRANSFER OF EMBRYO
Using ultrasound to guide placement, the embryo is transferred to the uterus using a long, thin catheter.

❽ VITRIFICATION
Unused human eggs and embryos are frozen rapidly, or vitrified, for possible future use by the parent.

**AMMA ELIAN
AND TWINS**
Amma's husband, Anwar, was
arrested in 2003 and sentenced
to life imprisonment. Denied
physical contact, Palestinian
political prisoners use IVF
to conceive children.

**'IVF FOR ALL'
PROTEST**
Until 2021, when there was
a change in French law,
*'procréation médicale
assistée'* (PMA) was denied
to single French women
and lesbian couples.

OCTOMOM
Nadya Suleman gave birth
to octuplets in January 2009
as a result of IVF. Nadya is
pictured here with octuplets
Josiah, Noah, Isaiah, Jonah,
Jeremiah, Makai, Maliyah
and Nariyah in 2013.

twin children into the world. However, the financial expense associated with some procedures, and the rates of success some people encounter, means that IVF twins are born to particular people in specific geographic locations.

Multiples, and particularly twins, can be a thrilling outcome for parents who have waited years to conceive. Long, expensive, complicated and painful fertility journeys can conclude with twins, or not. The media offer salacious stories of 'IVF tourists' who travel to warm cities with affordable or low-cost reproductive services.[8]

Economic cost is one consideration, as are the ethical, religious and legal codes of different cultures and countries; the availability of services based on age, marital status and sexual orientation; and the techniques and expertise required, free from fears that they will be of low quality or high risk. This has made some cities 'hubs' in terms of high-quality healthcare (Brussels, Barcelona, Los Angeles, Sydney, Singapore and Dubai). But they exist in a broader context. Surrogacy and donation are tightly regulated in Norway, Germany and the UK, while surrogacy and donation are prohibited in Spain and Italy. Since 2021, France has allowed lesbian and single women to access reproductive technologies, treatments and services.[9] Medical choice, trustworthiness and perceptions of enhanced quality are essential to those looking for donor eggs and sperm at any cost. For this reason, people travel all over the world to gain control over decisions with unpredictable outcomes.

Throughout the 1990s and 2000s, and thanks to ART, twin births became associated with celebrity wealth and access to private healthcare. An eclectic mix of celebrities have publicized the twin outcomes of their fertility treatments, including former US president George Bush Jnr and his wife Laura, Celine Dion, Jennifer Lopez, Angelina Jolie and Brad Pitt, John Legend and Chrissy Teigen, footballer Cristiano Ronaldo and the world's richest person, Elon Musk. Equating twins and material riches enters twins into the spectacular economics of wealth inequalities.

How twins are born and how many twins are born has changed rapidly. In 2006, Maria del Carmen Bousada sold her house to raise the $59,000 she needed for fertility treatment in the United States using donated sperm and eggs. She deceived the clinic about her age, and at 66 years and 358 days she became the world's oldest mother to give birth. 'I think everyone should become a mother at the right time for them,' she said when the twins were born.[10] She died three years later. In 2009, Nadya Suleman, already the mother of one set of IVF twins, gave birth to octuplets (six boys and two girls). All survived birth. She is better known in the US press as 'Octomom'. Suleman launched a media career that sought to both assetize and survive public opinion. Opportunistic media companies portrayed her as a sexual spectacle – ungodly, amoral and untrustworthy – unaware they were responding to a deep, cross-cultural tradition that condemns the mothers of twins.

The birth of IVF octuplets also sparked an overdue debate about regulations and practices in US clinical fertility centres. The doctor treating her lost his medical licence because he had knowingly transferred twelve frozen embryos left from her previous

JIMMY AND JEY USO
Part of the Anoaʻi wrestling
family, the Uso twins are mirror
twins. Pictured here in 2016,
they have performed together
as a tag-team since 2010.

WINKLEVOSS TWINS
Mirror twins Tyler (right) and
Cameron Winklevoss, pictured
rowing on the Thames in 2010,
are former international rowers
and now entrepreneurs.

stimulated IVF cycles, which the medical board of California found to be 'life-threatening practice'.[11] The thresholds of risk are assessed after the fact. None of Suleman's children died as a consequence of her fertility treatment. However, many mothers, foetuses and newborn children have encountered health and economic challenges as a direct (and indirect) consequence of accessing fertility treatments. While some see ART-born twins as potent symbols of technology, fertility and consumer choice, others make a counterclaim: twin conceptions and births are dangerous, and they should be avoided wherever possible.

When the first IVF twins were born in the early 1980s, they were premature and experienced congenital health problems that meant they needed weeks of hospital treatment. Multiple births are risky in modern medical terms, just as they have been in previous eras. Twins increase the rates of maternal and infant death, premature birth, pre-eclampsia, developmental delay and pre-term delivery, and they double the rates of physical and cognitive disabilities. Twins also require extra care, which isolates parents and carers and exacerbates financial and other difficulties. One leading clinician described multiple births as 'the single biggest risk to the health and welfare of children before and after IVF'. A British review of ART pregnancies in the early 2000s found that hundreds of multiple births resulted in stillborn or terminally ill infants.

Countries in Europe, and increasingly in North America, now aim to reduce multiple-embryo transfer. They encourage what are sometimes called 'one at a time' policies.

These drastically reduce the chances of twin births, but can be frustrating to prospective parents who are desperate to conceive and will go to almost any cost to improve their chances. For the first time since twin birth rates began to increase in the 1980s, they are now flattening out or decreasing in Europe and North America. In the United States, the number of twin births doubled from 1980 (68,339) to 2014 (135,336), peaking in 2007 (138,961), but the 123,536 twin births in 2018 was the lowest number reported since 2002.[12] The less-regulated era of ART twinning is unlikely to be over, and the practice is being offshored to clinics and countries where regulations are less strict or money makes regulations no impediment.

Since the late 1990s, researchers have been refining the tools they can use to scan, sequence and dissect different parts of twin people. There are many other biological sub-types of twin. Mirror twins (sometimes called 'mirror-image' twins) are a type of monozygotic twin with identically opposite features: for example, their dominant hands might contrast, with one twin using their left and the other their right for most activities. Their hair may grow in asymmetric whorls on different sides of their heads, or they may have birthmarks on different limbs. Mirror twins are usually identified and categorized based on their visible physical features, but there is no universal test, and differences may be internal, too. For example, when Lucas and Louie Cooke were born by emergency caesarean in Britain in 2013, they were premature and underweight, and needed weeks of hospital care before their parents could take them home. Following tests,

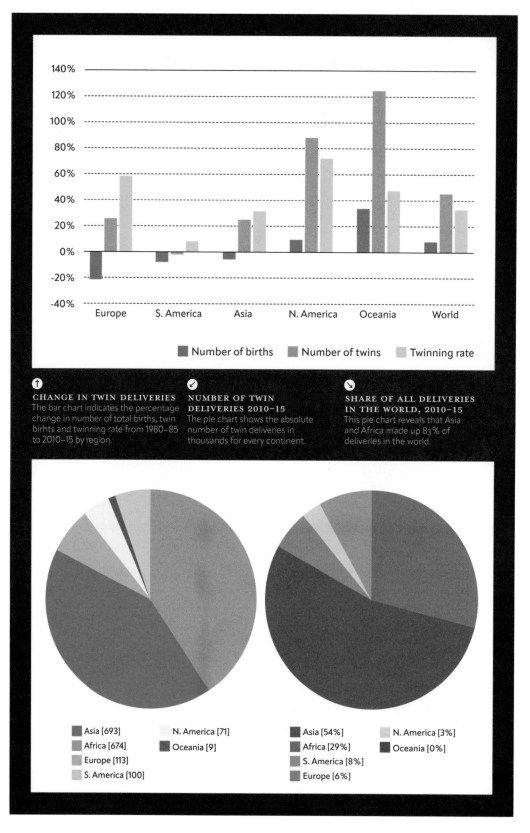

CHANGE IN TWIN DELIVERIES
The bar chart indicates the percentage change in number of total births, twin birhts and twinning rate from 1980–85 to 2010–15 by region.

NUMBER OF TWIN DELIVERIES 2010–15
The pie chart shows the absolute number of twin deliveries in thousands for every continent.

SHARE OF ALL DELIVERIES IN THE WORLD, 2010–15
This pie chart reveals that Asia and Africa made up 83% of deliveries in the world.

Number of births   Number of twins   Twinning rate

Asia [693]   N. America [71]
Africa [674]   Oceania [9]
Europe [113]
S. America [100]

Asia [54%]   N. America [3%]
Africa [29%]   Oceania [0%]
S. America [8%]
Europe [6%]

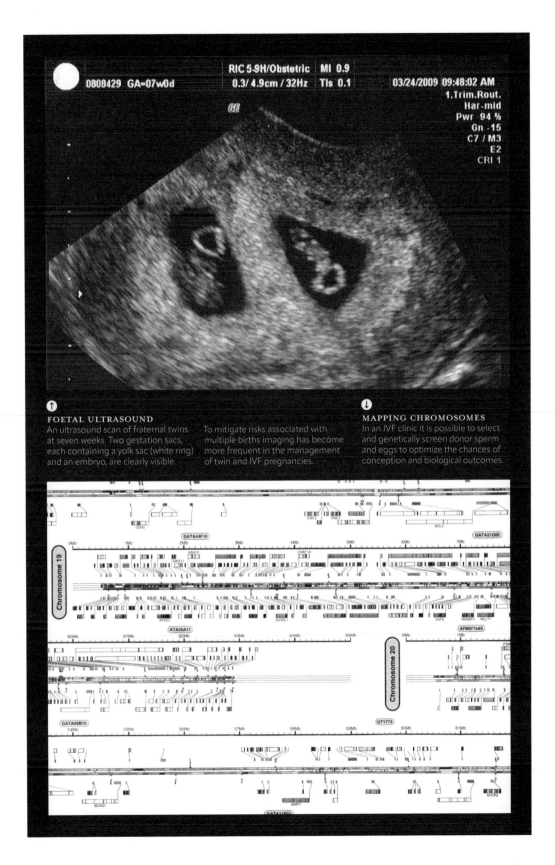

FOETAL ULTRASOUND

An ultrasound scan of fraternal twins at seven weeks. Two gestation sacs, each containing a yolk sac (white ring) and an embryo, are clearly visible.

To mitigate risks associated with multiple births imaging has become more frequent in the management of twin and IVF pregnancies.

MAPPING CHROMOSOMES

In an IVF clinic it is possible to select and genetically screen donor sperm and eggs to optimize the chances of conception and biological outcomes.

doctors explained that Lucas's heart, liver and spleen were in the opposite side of his body. Fortunately, this mirroring was not life threatening.

Lucas and Louie reflect an uncertainty (and another source of fascination) connected to mirror twins. How many twins are born with interior differences? Some propose that as many as 25 per cent of monozygotic twins are mirror twins, but this is just an estimate. We do not know. Mirror twins happen at a late-stage separation, between seven and ten days after the embryo is fertilized. They carry the marks of this late separation, the closest to being and yet not being conjoined. They suggest another way of thinking about the making of twins that sidelines visual similarity. If monozygotic are 'clones' of each other, they are not equally so. Their mirrored features are produced by similar genetics and opposite outcomes.

The idea of being born genetically identical is no longer unusual. The first genetically identical clones and twin clones were bioengineered at Scotland's Roslin Institute in July 1995. Sheep Megan and Morag were cloned from different cells and paved the way for the laboratory's more famous clone, Dolly the Sheep, whose creation was announced in 1997. Megan and Morag demonstrated that a sheep can be created using adult cells transferred into the nucleus of another cell – a technical practice that made the Dolly experiment possible. Now that cloning was a practical reality, legislators moved to set more specific laws to prohibit human cloning. Monozygotic twins were often used to test limits of what was acceptable. Legal scholars and government policy advisors argued that clones and monozygotic twins were treated as genetic equals, but twins are spared the cruel consequences of knowing their genetic futures. As they tried to regulate the future of human cloning, policymakers argued clones have derivative lives – hostages rather than agents over their futures.[13]

National legal codes governing scientific activity often rely on scientists regulating one another through institutional systems of professional training, accreditation and peer review. But the reality is much closer to Hollywood fiction. In a world of science and twins, there seems always to be shock and surprise close at hand. In November 2018, Chinese scientist He Jiankui (b. 1984) appeared before the global media to announce the birth of Lulu and Nana, twin children secretly made thanks to a controversial experiment using a gene-editing technique called CRISPR-Cas9. Editing the core part of the human genome or 'germline' DNA has not been outlawed by international agreement, but many nations have laws that prohibit it. He led the experiment to bioengineer embryos because, he said, one parent was affected by HIV and the gene-editing technology could lessen Lulu and Nana's vulnerability to HIV. He was later jailed. Critics argued over the experiment's justification and the influence it may have on global agreements used to limit controversial technologies. Regardless, the world's first genetically modified humans are twins, redefining how humans modify their species. ✼✼

CLONED SHEEP, 1997
Dolly was the first mammal to be cloned from an adult somatic cell, using the process of nuclear transfer.

CLONED PIGS, 2000
Millie, Christa, Alexis, Carrel and Dotcom were the world's first cloned pigs, shown in a pen in Virginia.

CLONED GOATS, 2003
Four cloned goats displayed at the Shanghai Wild Animal Park on the outskirts of China's financial hub.

CLONED COWS, 2003
Genetically identical copies of the first ever cloned cow, which are heavier than calves conceived naturally.

the Dolly sisters

Landa -
Paris

PART THREE

❁ ❁

SPECTACLE + PROPHECY

VII.   Born Entertainers

— ❆ ❆ —

The idea of twinship as a visually enchanting puzzle is Shakespeare's theme in *The Comedy of Errors* (c. 1594). It features two sets of identical and identically named twins. Antipholus has lost his brother in a shipwreck and vows to find him. In the process of them being reunited, the play captures something spectacular about seeing look-alike twins. It also examines the psychological perils of being a twin divided. On setting out on his quest, Antipholus says:

> I to the world am like a drop of water
> That in the ocean seeks another drop,
> Who, falling there to find his fellow forth,
> Unseen, inquisitive, confounds himself.

Feeling confounded, seeking a person he also takes himself to be: 'So I, to find a mother and a brother, / In quest of them, unhappy, lose myself.' Characters like Antipholus fear they live the double bind of desire and loss, suffer the incomplete life of a twinless twin or risk it all searching for an identical other they may never find.

Shakespeare used fictional twins to pose questions about what life, death and freedom might mean to his audiences. After a lot of confusion and mishap, the twins in *The Comedy of Errors* face each other – stupefied with joy and amazement, entertained to at last capture the other's desire. They see the possibility of recognizing themselves anew: 'Methinks you are my glass, and not my brother: / I see by you I am a sweet-faced youth.' Mixed-sex twins Sebastian and Viola in *Twelfth Night* (c. 1601–02) also meet in a final scene of recognition and the Duke (with whom Viola is in love) cannot untangle them: 'One face, one voice, one habit, and two persons, / A natural perspective that is and is not.' These may be works of comedic confusion, but an existential mystery furnishes each marvel with malevolence, a sinister sense that nature has been, or can be, undone.

Shakespeare's twin comedies are revolutionary. Each suggests the sudden disappearance of solid reality, including the material certainty of twin people and the categories we use to make sense of them. All the while, twins can stand for what is true and real. They produce evidence that cannot be faked. You can be a canny actor or a clown, but you cannot fake a twin. Or can you? Unlike other mythic creatures, twins pass in and out of fictional worlds. Indeed, what we fancy twins to be is integral to their history. For example, no one has determined the true identity of the masked man incarcerated in France until his death in 1703, a prisoner of state during the time of Louis XIV (1638–1715). Long after he died, he remained the subject of great speculation. The French philosopher Voltaire (1694–1778) argued that the prisoner was the king's illegitimate older brother. In the final part of Alexandre Dumas's (1802–70) popular *d'Artagnan Romances* (1847–50), 'the

ROSIE AND JENNY DOLLY
Promotional poster for 'The Dolly Sisters', created in France, c. 1925. Twin acts who could sing, dance or act were very popular during the early 20th century.

LEIF AND PAAL ROSCHBERG
'The Rocky Twins', pictured here in 1926 dressed as sailors, were Jazz Age stars of the stage and screen. One of their popular acts involved dressing in drag to imitate the Dolly Sisters.

⇈ / ↑
ROBSON AND CRANE
Stuart Robson and William H. Crane had a long relationship playing comic duos in London and New York. They are featured here in posters advertising the Broadway production of *The Comedy of Errors* (c. 1879) in which they starred.

⇑ / ↑

TWEEDLEDUM AND TWEEDLEDEE
Illustrations by John Tenniel from *Through the Looking Glass* (1871) by Lewis Carroll. Originally characters in a nursery rhyme, the twins declare a fight, are scared by a passing crow and forget their quarrel. Alice helps them repeat this routine.

man in the iron mask' is imagined as the king's identical twin. He is kept locked up for the safety of crown and state. The saga concludes with a thwarted conspiracy to swap king for twin – all possible as long as no one knows that the king has a look-alike brother. Now, semi-detached from its historical source, spiralling away into literary and cinematic history, the idea of the dangerous twin continues to threaten social orders. It must be repressed. And so the drama of this repression remains a source of both pleasure and horror.

Works of fiction that reveal or simply revel in the eerie qualities attached to twins can unsettle the natural world. This is part of the appeal of a classic work of American Gothic, *The Fall of the House of Usher* (1839) by Edgar Allan Poe (1809–49). It tells of Roderick and Madeline Usher, who share 'strange sympathies of a scarcely intelligible nature ...'.[1] Having fallen ill, Madeline appears to die. Roderick and the narrator bury her in the family tomb but Roderick is haunted by his sister. She later reappears to have revenge on him for burying her alive. The twins die together, and their house and dynasty collapse in convulsion.

The worlds of literary twins can be unpredictable and, therefore, artistically useful. Mark Twain's *The Prince and the Pauper* (1881) temporarily swaps the lives of two boys of the same age and physical likeness, allowing readers to imagine alternatives to a 'natural' social hierarchy. They can disturb the simple realist divide between fiction and reality, as in the detective short story *The Twins* (1924) by Japanese writer Tarō Hirai (1894–1965), known by the pen name Edogawa Ranpo. Here, one twin murders his brother and takes over his life, job, family, house and all. Or in the centrifugal, revolutionary wordplay of *Finnegans Wake* (1939) by James Joyce (1882–1941) or Ágota Kristóf's (1935–2011) postmodern trilogy *Le Grand Cahier* (1986), *La Preuve* (1988) and *Le Troisième Mensonge* (1991). Twins are the accomplice characters of 20th-century literary experiments, used to test the interdependent thresholds of reason, sensation and madness.

Interest in the life and death struggles of twins has been key in the development of the US entertainment industry, starting with the sideshow in the 19th century. This spectacle underpinned the commercial exploitation of conjoined twins and their ability to financialize their lives. Chang and Eng Bunker from Siam (modern-day Thailand) coined the term 'Siamese twins' to market themselves. They first toured with the merchants that found them in Siam, going from town to city and staying in local hotels, inviting visitors to their 'freak show'. Though their early exhibitions emphasized their exoticness in terms of dress and behaviour, they soon gained their independence, later naturalized as American citizens, and settled as landholders, husbands, and slaveowners. They were eager to present themselves (along with their twenty-one children) in conversation with guests.[2] How they showed audiences the anomaly of a conjoined life developed, as their place in society changed.

After their international success, capitalizing on their disability and racial otherness, the term 'Siamese' was then applied to other conjoined people. When Kate Skinner, an unmarried British barmaid, gave birth to conjoined twins Daisy and Violet, a pub landlady bought and displayed them. They became indentured to a series of owners. These twins also travelled the world, calling

---

❶/❷
INTRA-CLASS DOUBLE
Illustrations by William Hatherell from the 1909 edition of Mark Twain's novel *The Prince and the Pauper* (1881). Pauper Tom Canty and Edward Tudor were born on the same day and look identical. After meeting accidentally, the prince invites Tom into his palace chamber and they decide to swap clothes to discover what it would be like to live as the other.

❸/❹
UNCANNY DOUBLES
Illustrations by Byam Shaw from the 1909 edition of *Selected Tales of Mystery* by Edgar Allan Poe. The first shows twins Roderick and Madeline Usher from the short story *The Fall of* the House of Usher (1839) in a state of near death. The second shows William Wilson and his double at a carnival in Rome, from the eponymous short story (1839).

DEATH OF THE DOUBLE
Illustration by Harry Clarke depicting William Wilson fatally stabbing his double in the climax of the story 'William Wilson' from a 1923 edition of Edgar Allan Poe's selected short stories. In killing his double he kills himself.

TRANSFORMATION
Illustration by S. G. Hulme Beaman depicting Dr Jekyll in the midst of one of his transformations into Mr Hyde in a 1930 edition of the Gothic novella *Strange Case of Dr Jekyll and Mr Hyde* (1886) by Robert Louis Stevenson.

REMARKABLE HUMAN PHENOMENA!

THE AFRICAN TWINS

(CHRISTINA AND MILLY,)

These extraordinary Children, only Five Years old, and where Nature has linked by an Indissoluble Band, about 16 inches in circumference, having excited the most intense interest, and created the greatest sensation wherever they have been witnessed, will be ON VIEW, for a brief period only, at the

EGYPTIAN HALL,
PICCADILLY,
On MONDAY, Sept. 15, 1855,
AND FOLLOWING DAYS,
FROM 2 TILL 4, AND FROM 6 TILL 8 O'CLOCK.

They where born in Slavery ; and their Guardian, appointed by the Orphan Court of Philadelphia, United States, legally apprenticed them to Mr. THOMPSON, of that City, who instantly freed them from their degrading Bondage and determined to appreate the Receipts arising from their Public Exhibition to the purpose of financipating the Parents of the Children, who are at this moment Slaves on a North-American Plantation. The better feelings of Humanity, as well as the strongest impulses of Curiosity, are therefore to be jointly gratified by their inspection. As already stated on the Public Prints, they were felicitously abducted from the Bedford Head, Covent Garden, by the man who had charge of them, and recovered in Dundee, Scotland ; the Scottish Authorities, as well as the Metropolitan Magistracy, having taken the warmest interest in their abduction.

Unlike most of these Enormities of Nature that have been heretofore exhibited, these

INTERESTING CHILDREN

have an eminently Pleasing and Attractive Appearance, and their Extraordinary Conformation causes led to delight as well as to astonish every Visitor. They sing, with wonderful precision, the Native Melodies of their own Country, and thus the unparalleled circumstance of a Duet, arising from Two Voices, but originating in the division of One Mind, may be said to form the last, greatest, and most exciting Novelty EVER YET RECORDED in the ANNALS of the MARVELLOUS.

The immediate attention of the Public to this Announcement is earnestly solicited, as they are now en route to the French Capital, where they have received a Special Invitation, and will thence return to Philadelphia to complete their Filial Mission.

To be seen Living
AT THE
EGYPTIAN HALL,
PICCADILLY.
THE
LANCASHIRE
PRODIGY
THIS EXTRAORDINARY
MALE CHILD!

Having **FOUR HANDS, FOUR ARMS, FOUR LEGS,** and **FOUR FEET,** with **TWO BODIES,** and only **ONE HEAD,**
Each body performing the Ordinary function of Nature independent of the other.

He was BORN at STALEY BRIDGE

Near Manchester, May 27th, 1837, and may be seen Alive with its Mother in an Healthy State, as above, from 11 till 2, & from 3 till 6

ADMISSION 1s. EACH.
N.B.—A PRIVATE ROOM FOR LADIES

J. W PEEL, Printer, 9, New Cut, Lambeth

TO THE CURIOUS!!!
PATRONIZED BY THE FACULTY.
The greatest Phenomenon of Human Nature ever exhibited to the Public!!!

Two Children
UNITED

From the Umbilical Chord to the top of the Breast-Bone.
BORN ALIVE, January, 1833.
ALLOWED BY THE FACULTY
FAR TO SURPASS THE
Siamese Twins.

This Phenomenon opens a wide field for inquiry to the Members of the Medical Profession; its perfection astonishes every beholder.

THE
MATCHLESS LAMB

With three bodies (two of which denote the Male, the other the Female), eight legs, and only one Head, fell the 1st of May last, at Mr. R. Pittis's, Winering, Hants.

This also stands Unrivalled ; it bids defiance, even to Record, to cope with its wonderful Structure.

WONDERFUL KANGAROO PIG.

With no fore legs, two behind these being double jointed, there being four joints in each, a double act of teeth, and no eyes.

The curious and Learned must be astonished at the perfection, symmetry, and beauty of these unaccountable productions of Nature. It must be seen to be appreciated.

The PROPRIETOR begs to say, he challenges the WORLD for 1000 Guineas, for such productions of Nature. The Public are respectfully cautioned not to listen to the evil and ill-disposed assertions made by a scurrious Exhibitor of Models against this Exhibition, but to satisfy themselves by strictly examining these Matchless productions of Nature.

To the above is added a fine View of the
FATAL CONVICT SHIP, AMPHITRITE,
N.B.—No Wax-work. No Models in this Collection. No Deception.

Printed particulars may be had at the place of Exhibition, No. 23, High Street, Bloomsbury

Hows and Thornton, Printers, 11, Warren Street, Middlesex Hospital.

Great living phenomenon,
THE
BROTHERS TOCCI.

Extraordinary living curiosity.

More remarkable than the Siamese Twins.

More interesting than the Sisters Millie-Christine.

Extraordinary living curiosity.

More remarkable than the Siamese Twins.

More interesting than the Sisters Millie-Christine.

CURIOUS HISTORY OF THE
Life, Habits, and Adventures of that Strangely-formed Being, and Singular-looking Creature, the
BABOON LADY,
MISS JULIA PASTRANA

Known as the "Nondescript," exhibiting at the Regent Gallery.
Her Remarkable Formation, and Mysterious Parentage, and how she was
Discovered in a Cave, suckled by her Indian Mother,
DWELLING ONLY WITH BABOONS, BEARS, AND MONKEYS.

WITH A FULL DESCRIPTION OF THE WONDERFUL
LIVE TWO-IN-ONE, OR,
DOUBLE-BODIED BOY!
At Dr. Kahn's Museum; including the Cause of those Curiosities of Nature.
PRICE ONE PENNY.
BURROWS, Printer, 15, Old Street Road.

PICCADILLY HALL

EXTRAORDINARY ATTRACTION! Commencing
TUESDAY AFTERNOON, FEB. 17th 1885

Engagement of the Greatest Living Curiosity the World has ever produced:

MISS
MILLIE CHRISTINE
THE CAROLINA TWIN.

NOW ON HER
Farewell Tour,
So 'tis your last opportunity of seeing her

2 HEADS, 4 ARMS, 4 FEET,
All in One Perfect Body Meet.

Two Heads with but a single thought,
Two hearts that beat as one.

None like me since the days of Eve
None such perhaps shall ever live

Walks ON 2 or 4 FEET

SHE SINGS WITH BOTH MOUTHS.

TWO RECEPTIONS DAILY
FASHIONABLE Afternoon Reception
FROM 2 TILL 5. ADMISSION, 2s. CHILDREN, 1s.
EVENING, FOR THE GENERAL PUBLIC,
FROM 7 TILL 9. HALF-PRICE.
ADULTS, 1s. CHILDREN, 6d.

FINELY EDUCATED, REFINED, and ACCOMPLISHED. CHEERFUL, AMIABLE and HAPPY.

THEY DANCE ON 4 FEET.

THE FAMOUS TWO
HEADED NIGHTINGALE

Miss MILLIE CHRISTINE, the World's Wonder, was born in 1851, is now 33 years old. The lady has travelled throughout the civilised world, and attracted more universal attention from all classes than any other human being that has ever existed.
"From the Crowned Heads of Every Court in Europe" to the humblest Peasant, the Great and Small of the Earth pronounce Miss MILLY CHRISTINE, "THE LADY WITH TWO HEADS," to be the
THE MOST MARVELLOUS EXHIBITION EVER WITNESSED.
ENGAGED AT THE ENORMOUS SALARY of 1000 dollars (£200) PER WEEK, the largest sum ever paid to any LIVING CURIOSITY
TO APPEAR TWICE DAILY, IN CONJUNCTION WITH

HARVEY'S MIDGES
THE SMALLEST PEOPLE IN THE WORLD, and
Liliputian Choir, forming the Most Extraordinary Combination of Living Wonders, AND UNIQUE AND CHARMING ENTERTAINMENTS EXTANT.

Both Exhibitions and Liliputian Concert Company in the Same Hall, Same Time, and ONE PRICE OF ADMISSION TO SEE ALL.

AUBERT'S Steam Printing Works, 11, Maiden Lane, Strand.

PICCADILLY HALL.

THE WORLD'S WONDER!
Miss Millie Christine.

TWO RECEPTIONS DAILY.
Afternoon 2 till 5. Evening 7 till 9.

Two smiles with but a single thought,
Two hearts that beat as one.

None like me since the day of Eve,
None such perhaps shall ever live.

THE
TWO-HEADED NIGHTINGALE,
AND
HARVEY'S MIDGES
THE Smallest People in the World.
[P.T.O.

PATRONIZED BY THE FACULTY.

The Greatest Phenomenon of Human Nature ever exhibited to the Public!!!

TWO CHILDREN UNITED
From the Umbilical Cord to the top of the Breast-bone,
BORN ALIVE JANUARY, 1833,
ALLOWED BY THE FACULTY
FAR TO SURPASS THE
SIAMESE TWINS,
ARE NOW EXHIBITING AT
THE ROTUNDA,
BLACKFRIARS ROAD,
From Nine in the Morning till Ten in the Evening.

It opens a wide field for inquiry to the Members of the Medical Profession. The curious and learned must be astonished at the perfection, symmetry, and beauty of this unaccountable production of Nature.

Printed Particulars of these Phenomenon may be had at the place of exhibition.

J. W. PEEL, Printer, 9, New Cut, Lambeth.

WONDERFUL NATURAL PHENOMENON!
TO BE SEEN

At No. 107, Regent Street,
A CHILD
With Two Faces, Four Eyes, Two Mouths, Two Noses, Two Ears, and Two Chins,

All in perfect Nature; different coloured Hair, with only one Head and Body; Hands and Feet as exact as any other Child, and there is nothing in it unpleasant to the sight of any beholder. The said Child was born at Taunton, in the County of Somerset, on the 23d of December, 1827.
The Child is the Daughter of JOSEPH and ELIZABETH VERRIER, who will exhibit it at the place above-mentioned, or at any Lady's or Gentleman's House, if required.

Admittance—ONE SHILLING.

J. SALE, Printer, 15, Union Street, Borough New Town.

FIRST TOUR IN GREAT BRITAIN.
DURING THE FAIR.
£1,000
CHALLENGE TO THE WORLD!
TO PRODUCE the EQUAL OF LALLOO, the GREATEST LIVING
WONDER IN THE WORLD!
A Native of Lucknow, Central India,

LALLOO

LALLOO   LALLOO

A very Intelligent, Strange, and most Remarkable
INDIAN BOY!
Seventeen Years of Age. He Stands Five Feet in Height.
Lalloo has Two Perfect Bodies
Lalloo has Four Perfect Arms
Lalloo has Four Perfect Hands
Lalloo has Four Perfect Legs
Lalloo has Four Perfect Feet
BUT LALLOO HAS ONLY GOT
ONE PERFECT HEAD
IN FACT, IT IS SIMPLY
A BOY and GIRL Joined together
And if LALLOO is not really
ALIVE
£100
WILL BE GIVEN TO ANY CHARITABLE INSTITUTION.

NOTE:—This is really the most Marvellous Freak of Nature Living, that has ever been made a Public Exhibition of in this, or any other Country, and is a Novelty that every Father and Mother ought to see.

REMARKS.
Of the Medical Scientific Papers, and certain Learned Societies and others, about the Boy LALLOO, as follows:—"He is nothing less than a Marvel, compared to which the Two-Headed Nightingale, and the Siamese Twins were as nothing."
"Without a parallel in the World's History."—Dr. Thomas GREGSON, M.B. Surgeon
A Clergyman says:—"There are Fourteen Thousand Millions of People in this World, he he's the only one of his kind that has been alive."

He has been Exhibited in the Portland Hall, Langham Place, London, at the Admission of One Shilling Each.

JAMES NORMAN and M. D. FRANCIS, Proprietors.

CONJOINED TWINS SHOWS
These handbills and posters (1830–90) testify to the
popularity of conjoined twins as exhibits in international
touring shows. London's Egyptian Hall, Piccadilly, hosted
many such acts from America and Europe.

THE PYGOPAGI TWINS
Poster advertising the appearance of conjoined twins
Josepha and Rosalie Blazek at the Egyptian Hall, London,
in 1880. They were also known as the 'Bohemian'
twins owing to patronage by the Empress of Austria.

↓

CHANG AND ENG
Colour engraving by Hugh S. Miller, depicting conjoined
twins Chang and Eng – the original Siamese twins. Born
in 1811 they were exhibited in England in 1829, toured
Europe twice and settled in America. They died in 1874.

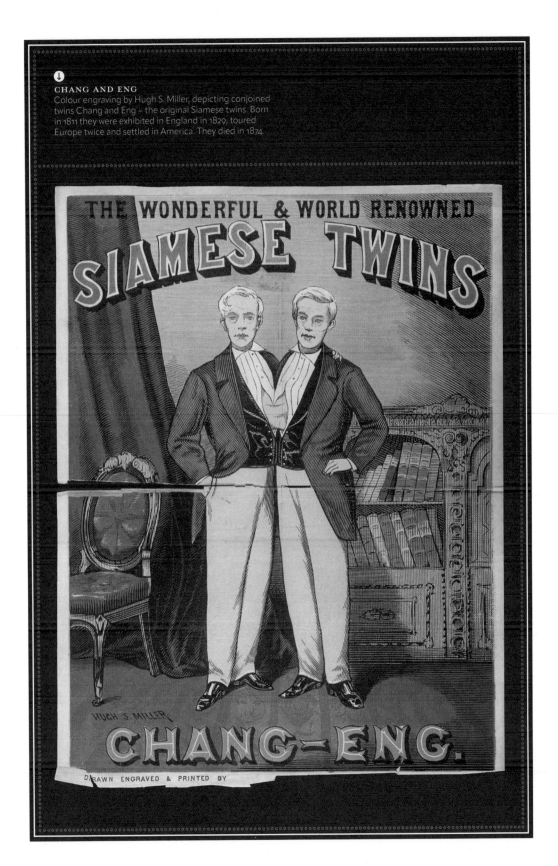

themselves the Siamese Twins, the Hilton Sisters and the Brighton Twins – and later the San Antonio Twins when they moved to the United States.

Violently abused throughout their working lives, the twin's earliest memories involved pub visitors lifting their skirts to examine their bodies. Their tours of vaudeville and burlesque stages during the 1920s only made money for their legal owners, and the twins performed under the constant threat of violence and institutionalization. At the advice of Harry Houdini they sought their emancipation, which they gained in 1931.

By necessity and a desire to take control of their destinies, Chang and Eng sought opportunities to earn money, travel the world, socialize and meet leading medical professionals.[3] In turn, the material relation of being conjoined gave twins a geopolitical significance. Throughout the 19th century, twins and conjoined twins were used as rhetorical figures of speech by politicians, journalists and satirists to describe imperial dependencies, interdependencies and other codependent relationships.

With the rise of vaudeville and the explosion of theatre revue in the early 20th century, twins such as Rosie and Jenny Dolly became international stars of the stage. They and others mark the beginning of an era of twin celebrity. Originally from Hungary, the Dolly Sisters performed feather-clad, sequinned routines on Broadway in *Ziegfeld Follies*. Singing and dancing in unison when they auditioned for Ziegfeld, he is said to have been unimpressed by their skill but admiring of their physical appearance: 'You can't do much, but you're cute.' Wildly popular,

especially with wealthy men, the Dolly Sisters led fabulous lives on and off stage until their union was cut short. Jenny sustained life-changing injuries after a car accident in 1933. Her physical and mental health deteriorated, and her social and stage career was over. Jenny took her own life in 1941. And yet the commercial demand and platform for high-energy look-alike twins was up and running. Callous and opportunistic interest in twin performers and the sexual fantasies they inspired in audiences meant that many more feathered, high-kicking twins were on hand to delight the crowds. Chief among these were the exuberant Leif and Paal Roschberg, known as 'the Rocky Twins'. They were said to be 'so ravishing that each night after the show they would allow themselves to be kidnapped by beauty enthusiasts of both sexes'.[4]

As twins became brands – their names lit up on Broadway billboards – twin people became a brand's best friend. They started to be used as a playful visual way of catching consumer attention, flattering the purchaser's power to discern and cultivate good sense. Commodities sell for being reliable, common, rare, standard or bespoke; occasionally, they are all these things and more. The advertising industry has used twins to tell the real McCoy from cheap fakes and imitations. The ad man's attempt to make the buyer feel wise can mean twins enter a psychological game. Against the threat of absolute imitation, advertiser and customer stand together in solidarity in the interests of choice. Yet duplication of the product or service is integral to economic success. For some brands, twin people are representative of a reassuring duplication of two things that gives guarantees against lowly

THE SISTERS G

An internationally famous dance act from Berlin, Karla and Eleanor Gutöhrlein were known professionally as the 'Sisters G'. They were assumed to be twins, with their matching bobbed haircuts, but in fact differed in age by more than a year. They performed in several films, including *King of Jazz* (1930).

THE ROWE SISTERS

Identical twins Pauline and Betty Rowe, known as 'the Greyhounds of Paris', perform a dance routine in 1925. They danced regularly at the Casino de Paris and the Alhambra in Brussels from 1924 until Betty married French actor Henri Garat in 1932 and the pair stopped dancing professionally.

or unreliable proxies. In a world of commodity substitutes, capitalism has few rivals.[5]

The stage and screen make twins stock in trade, visual and dramatic gifts. They are evidence of an old system of folklore adapting to new media. Some modern representations of twins scarcely stray from the centuries-old tropes of myth, cosmology, medieval romance and religious veneration, with their madcap substitutions, mistaken identities, bed-trick swaps and miraculous reunions. Truthfulness and authenticity are key to these twinly presentations; twins provide the revelation of narrative truth and recognition. But twins are figures made up of many other people, and in them we find a model for all character performance: the requirement that characters have many personas, subtle and not so subtle representations formed from a chorus of other cultural projections.

The history of the cinema involves people pretending to be twins, single-born people without lived experience that strive to play up to what scriptwriters, directors, executives and their audiences expect from twin characters. Many representations of twinning are distributed: a collective achievement. Over and over, twins are put into mischief and misrule – placed into psychologically troubled, divided and disturbed situations in which they must survive.

Favourite plotlines – comic, thrilling and tragic – allow separated and later reunited actors to pass as siblings. For the past fifty years of film history, leading men and women have assumed twin identities and double parts. Cult classics such as *Sisters* (1972), featuring Margot Kidder (1948–2018) as twins Danielle Breton and Dominique Blanchion, and *Twins* (1988), with Arnold Schwarzenegger and Danny DeVito, use twins as dramatic devices to split, explore, develop and dissolve as a narrative spectacle. They can do so because audiences know actors play twins temporarily, as a form of work. Every twin is the narrative's prop and propeller. In *Big Business* (1988), a modern screen adaptation of Shakespeare's *The Comedy of Errors*, Bette Midler (b. 1945) plays separated twins Sadie Shelton and Sadie Ratliff, and Lily Tomlin (b. 1939) plays Rose Ratliff and Rose Shelton – two sets, divided at birth, and later reunited to the confusion of all. Ten years later, *The Parent Trap* (1998) revived the entertainment of twins raised apart and reunited, with a young Lindsay Lohan (b. 1989) making her Hollywood breakthrough as Hallie Parker and Annie James. These films have a wacky energy, partly because the audience knows that twins are being made before their eyes. We are asked to suspend our disbelief and accept that one person can multiply themselves. It often produces a skittish anarchy that not only raises the expectation that actual twins are mad, bad or both, but also inspires the madness that every individual has the ability to unlock in themselves. *Dead Ringers* (1988), starring Jeremy Irons (b. 1948) as the Mantle twins, was the first film to present an actor playing both twins on screen simultaneously, ensuring there is no telling where Irons/the Mantles begin or end. Jean-Claude Van Damme (b. 1960) in *Double Impact* (1991), Christian Bale (b. 1974) in *The Prestige* (2006) and Tom Hardy (b. 1977) in *Legend* (2015) all achieve a similar visual and hence psychological control, one that is often used to express or criticize male violence between twins.

To circulate in this media machine, twins go shoulder to shoulder. They express a physical

 LAUNDROMAT ADVERT
'America's Favorite Twins' feature in this Westinghouse laundromat 1951 advert.

 CALVERT ADVERT
The Collins twins appear in this 1953 advert for Calvert's gin and whisky.

 'WHAT A PAIR!'
The Corbett twins advertise 'best for you' Chesterfield cigarettes in 1954.

'TAREYTON TWOSOME'
Glamorous-looking twins advertise two types of Tareyton cigarettes in 1956.

 TWINDOW GLAZING
1958 advert for Twindow with twin girls playing with twin dolls.

 'ANGEL FACE' ADVERT
Advert for Pond's cosmetics from 1960 featuring twins.

AMONG THE LIVING
Albert Dekker plays the role of twins
John and Paul Raden in this 1941
American suspense thriller.

A STOLEN LIFE
Bette Davis stars as both twins Kate
and Patricia Bosworth in this 1946
film noir movie about a stolen identity.

⇑⇑ **THE DARK MIRROR**
Olivia de Havilland plays the role
of twins Terry and Ruth Collins
in this 1946 psychological thriller.

⇑ **ROSES ARE RED**
Peggy Knudsen and Patricia Knight
learn they have been tricked by
the same man in this 1947 movie.

1 1931

2 1937

3 1941

4 1946

5 1951

6 1956

7 1957

⇈ **ALEXA AND ALEXIE GRADY**
Lisa and Louise Burns star as the
Grady Twins – the iconic eerie twins
from horror movie *The Shining*, 1980.

↑ **ELLIOT AND BEVERLY MANTLE**
Jeremy Irons stars in *Dead Ringers* as twin
gynaecologists – a movie based on real
life twins Stewart and Cyril Marcus (1988).

DEMONIC TWINS
Jen and Sylvia Soska make a cameo
in *American Mary* (2012), the body
horror film they co-wrote and directed.

CLAUS AND LUCAS
András and László Gyémánt star as twins
in the film adaptation of *Le Grand Cahier*
(2013), the first in a trilogy of novels.

TIA AND TAMERA MOWRY
Stars of American series *Sister, Sister* (1994) and *Twitches* (2005), a movie about twin witches who are separated at birth. The twins went on to have their own reality series, *Tia & Tamera* (2011–13).

JAMES AND OLIVER PHELPS
The Phelps twins play Fred and George Weasley, the trickster twins of J. K. Rowling's *Harry Potter* books and film franchise. Pictured here behind the scenes of *Harry Potter and the Goblet of Fire* (2005).

or emotional companionship, rather than discord or outward conflict. For this reason, pictures of twins often display a measure of physical contact, reaffirmed by an intent look, preferably direct to camera, that they share in defiant confidence or self-knowledge. This is the regard that creates an opportunity to judge, to divide – an image whose symmetry seeks out the viewer to make one from two.

Images of twins are displayed in film and photography, as part of advertisements and publicity, in online and print news media, on television and in sports entertainment, as well as in fine art of every imaginable form. Each technology has been used to embrace twins and use them to embrace their viewers – to charm, captivate, seduce and sell. Twins respond by augmenting and elaborating on what they know and do, and how they appear.

Whether to create sameness or to be its compromise, directors and producers seek twin actors most alike in face and stature. They look for people who are able to inhabit a common set of postures and gestures, to speak in unison or give a punchline to jokes set up by their twin siblings. There are fine lines between humour and horror. Wearing identical dresses, Lisa and Louise Burns chant in unison as the chilling Grady sisters in *The Shining* (1980), fulfilling a horror genre that references novels such as *Brave New World* (1932) by Aldous Huxley (1894–1963) and *The Midwich Cuckoos* (1957) by John Wyndham (1903–69), as well as the 'freak' photography of Diane Arbus (1923–71). When twins are played by twin actors, another order of performance is found: an eerie sameness that makes a magic brand of family comedy, exemplified by James and

Oliver Phelps (b. 1986) as Fred and George Weasley in the *Harry Potter* films (2001–11), or lampooned by cartoon characters Patty and Selma in *The Simpsons* (1989–present). Synchrony and sameness are so prominent in screen depictions of twins that the collapse of very identical twin relations can be a source of great creative tension and mystery, as they are when Michael and Mark Polish (b. 1970) play conjoined twins Blake and Francis Falls in *Twin Falls Idaho* (1999).

Western visual media of the 20th century has generated an immense echo chamber of extreme resemblance on this basis, expelling unwanted twins who could not or would not make the grade. Twin actors in the adverts and films explored here are invariably white, young and able-bodied, and look similar. But the professional careers of twin entertainers can also be brief. Twin fame is lived conditionally. The entertainment industry ignores the vast majority of twins, particularly the large number of mixed-sex twins. Because their twins are not identical, the twin identities of Scarlett Johansson (b. 1984), Kiefer Sutherland (b. 1966) and Vin Diesel (b. 1967) are not well known. Only some have their twin status locked into their public life. The greatest twinless celebrity might be the King of Rock 'n' Roll himself, Elvis Presley (1935–77). Elvis was conceived as a twin and born with his stillborn brother, Jesse. Their mother, Gladys, told the young Elvis: 'When one twin died, the other one that lived got all the strength of both.'[6]

We learn something about being modern twins when we see twinship consumed by others: twinship is an identity that requires shared maintenance and a shared biography, but being a public twin is also to handle a delicate asset.

Twin models walk the runway as part of the Gucci Twinsburg Show at Milan Fashion Week in September 2022. Each pair of models is dressed in an identical outfit. Italian fashion designer Alessandro Michele was inspired by his mother and her twin sister when planning the show. He decided to feature sixty-eight sets of twins in his Twinsburg show.

New media technologies create opportunities for twins to loop content into different tides of attention. On social media, twin content producers and so-called 'twinfluencers' blend existing twin ideals – the legacy of traditional media – with emerging internet media technology. Collaborative pranks and tricks, dares and synchronized acrobatics are common. The visual language of twinning, now compressed and set to music, becomes a passport into a global market. Very young, predominately white, telegenic and athletic twin images hit this online economy, serving content based on the surveillance of user data. Recommendation algorithms respond to and direct users towards internet content that gets the most views, clicks, likes and shares. Popular twin personalities, such as the Stokes Twins, Rybka Twins or Dolan Twins, manipulate both the technological and historical patterns of what people want from twin people. Platforms host a particular variety of eccentric, bombastically 'zany' humour, played out between twins before their non-twin audiences. It recalls the slapstick comedies of the 1980s that preceded them but are unfamiliar to audiences in their teens and younger.[7] Twin folklore can spin again on another platform. Play can again be conflated with work. Twins become hard to prise apart from their professions in this environment, since being a twin is the thing being performed. Each money-making feature is presented as a twin feat.

We can see the rise of the twinfluencer as audience made and audience forming. Users and makers respond and anticipate each other's desires, with platforms providing feedback loops. Dynamic mimicry is key to how platforms make audiences into viewing groups. The internet appears to each of us based on our previous behaviours and the behaviours of others. According to how this information is collected and computed, social media platforms populate pages and feeds to optimize our engagement and promote our recurrent use. To do this, companies track our behaviour, match our data to other users like us and create temporary networks of similar (and dissimilar) people. In principle, the more data collected on how much we look at, click, scroll, stream and share different online features, the greater the aggregate ability will be to match our individualized profile to the profile of an 'ideal' viewer of an advertisement. In this sense, the internet's machinery is driven by phantoms and proxies that also financialize how twins appear online. The longer-term dream is to build fully synchronized data avatars, known as 'digital twins', used to simulate the future.

The ethics and legality of platform data collection, analysis and ad targeting are widely debated. Platforms, like twin acts, update but stay the same – creating incentives for twins to behave and see themselves in ways that are likely to make them visible to others like them, and to be liked by others. But if desires remain fixated on the cheerful sameness of twins, long established in 19th- and 20th-century media formats, then twins mediate little more than synchrony itself. Like other unsated appetites, the desire for twins is carefully and expertly trained via wide networks of other people who are also watching twins. Never before has the entertainment that can be taken from watching twin people spread so intricately into the digital networks of everyday life. ⌘⌘

VIII. Twins *and the* Paranormal

Strange and stranger coincidences between twins are almost limitless in number and variety. Not all can be enveloped by scientific explanation: a man becomes dizzy while his twin brother falls and is injured at work; an Italian woman experiences severe abdominal pain as her twin sister, thousands of miles away in Philadelphia, USA, goes into premature labour.[1] In Britain in 2009, Gemma Houghton had the feeling something was wrong with her sister Leanne. She ran to the bathroom and found Leanne unconscious in the bath, having an epileptic seizure. She saved her twin sister's life and national newspapers reported a psychic or 'sixth sense' connection.[2] Would these events repeat themselves for this pair or another? The question goes unanswered, for twins rarely step back into the limelight to perform the feat more than once. Instead, magical stories orbit like abandoned satellites, stripped of further reflection or conclusions.

In 1781, Methodist leader John Wesley (1703–91) recorded a dream shared between unnamed twin sisters that prevented a murder. One night, the sisters dreamt they were murdered by a resentful domestic servant. They woke and wrote to each other, learning that they dreamt the same dream, as did their father, on the same night. The servant was apprehended in possession of a knife and confessed his desire for revenge. Wesley himself heard this story as a rumour. He offered no religious interpretation or teaching. The story reflects on the strange power of twins to share each other's thoughts. Wesley remarked that the sisters had 'so strange a sympathy that if either of them is ill, or particularly affected at any time, the other is so likewise'.[3] Cast into a land of phantoms, apparitions and ghosts, these unknown twins also go untraced. Their true identity is historical guesswork.

As a storytelling tradition, supernatural twin tales might be seen as a kind of short story genre. Each psychic twin story is self-contained. Hard genetic determinists and ardent believers in twin telepathy share one thing in common: they view this behaviour as innate. Their stories stand alone. Each shows how the lives of twins converge. In form and content, this is a genre that is fundamentally gothic – formed through suggestive omissions and confused identities.

Paying some attention to the narrative forms taken by the twin psychic experience reveals how it can be used as a tactic of evasion or subterfuge. In his best-selling autobiography *Twin Ambitions* (2013), four-time British Olympic gold medallist Mo Farah (b. 1983) describes his relationship with his twin Hassan:

> Whenever Hassan is upset, or not feeling well, I'll somehow sense it. The same is true for Hassan when it comes to sensing how I feel. He'll just know when something isn't right with me. Then he'll pick up the phone and call me, ask how I am. Or I'll call him.[4]

The passage (and the book's title) suggests a twin relationship based on extrasensory honesty, compassion and self-disclosure.

TUNGA
Xifópagas Capilares Entre Nós (Capillary Xiphopagus Among Us), 1984, performance view. Twin adolescent girls stand in a warehouse, connected by their hair. The uncanny image is based on a Nordic myth about conjoined twins causing conflict in a village.

↑

DRESIE AND CASIE, TWINS,
WESTERN TRANSVAAL, 1993
Photograph of mute twins Dresie and Casie by Roger
Ballen (b. 1950) from the series *Platteland* (1986–93).
The series is a study of poor white communities
living on the edge of society in South Africa.

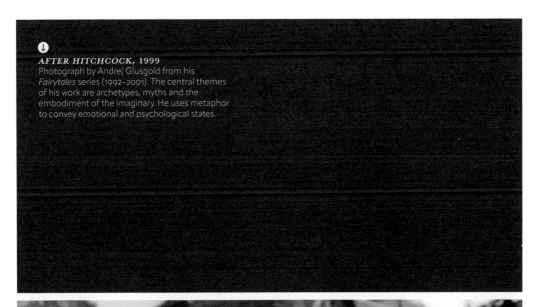

AFTER HITCHCOCK, 1999
Photograph by Andrej Glusgold from his
Fairytales series (1992–2001). The central themes
of his work are archetypes, myths and the
embodiment of the imaginary. He uses metaphor
to convey emotional and psychological states.

The 'Psychic Twins' are
pictured here identically
dressed, standing before
a window in an abandoned
house. The lighting and fabric
of the costumes make one
appear to merge with the other.

❈❈My sister and I ... were twins,
and you know how subtle are
the links which bind two souls
which are so closely aligned.❈❈

Arthur Conan Doyle, *The Adventure of the Speckled Band*, 1892

In 2022, Farah revealed that the first part
of his autobiography is fiction. He presented
his circumstance as a temporary separation
that was overcome by psychic empathy, but
Farah explained later that he was forcibly
separated from his brother and the rest
of his family, and he could not pick up the
phone. He was trafficked in Somalia as a
child and later forced into slavery in Britain.
The ambition and success that were previously
woven into Farah's twin relationship – the
magical capacity to think and feel with
someone thousands of miles away – also
obscured how or why that separation occurred.

Responses to unusual twins can be brutal.
June Gibbons (b. 1963) and her sister Jennifer
(1963–93) became known as 'The Silent Twins'.
They were singular in rural Wales in the 1970s
for being Black Caribbean twins who spoke to
no one. Taunted and racially abused, the twins
got into trouble with the police, who charged
them with petty crimes. Experts were baffled
by their behaviour, their fierce rejection of the
world and their interdependence. The Gibbons
were detained indefinitely in Broadmoor –
England's infamous psychiatric hospital.[5]
The twins understood that the only way to
escape captivity was for one of them to die.
After eleven years of imprisonment Jennifer
died, and June could begin to speak and to live.

Social theories of crime focus attention
on the racism and stigma experienced by
the Gibbons sisters. But social theories use
conventional boundaries of life and death
to make law, order and stigma meaningful.
Consider Joanna Pollock, eleven, and her
sister Jacqueline, six, who were killed in
a car accident in 1957. The following year,
their bereaved parents welcomed a set of

identical twin girls, Gillian and Jennifer. The
young girls appeared to recognize and recount
experiences unique to their dead sisters; they
had strong preferences for the sisters' toys and
they bore birthmarks that corresponded closely
to marks on Joanna and Jacqueline. Fearful of
cars, Gillian was heard to tell her sister: 'The
blood coming out of your eyes, that's where
the car hit you.' Their parents and parapsychic
investigators, including Hemendra Banerjee
and Ian Stevenson, concluded that the twins
were reincarnated spirits of their dead sisters,
and that they recalled 'Past Life Experiences'.[6]

Twin mysticism is not innocently supplied
or demanded. It can be manipulated by twins
and singletons alike. There exists a deep
willingness to invest hope in gifted twin people.
Linda and Terry Jamison, known as the 'Psychic
Twins', have developed a professional practice
and a large online following over the last
twenty-five years. Among 3,000 predictions
of events around the world, they claim to
have predicted the attacks on the World Trade
Center and the Pentagon on 11 September
2001.[7/8] The Jamisons believe in the general
goodness of their powers to spread benefits
to others. They have written four books,
including their autobiography, *Separated at
Earth: the Story of the Psychic Twins* and they
give readings on their YouTube channel.

Some twin pairs appear to be continuously
connected. Their experiences suggest a single
shared consciousness. 'Unnatural histories'
develop into cases such as that of Marta and
Silvia Landa, just four years old in 1976 and
living in Murillo de Río Leza, Spain. When
Marta fell sick with tonsillitis, her sister also
had a fever. When Marta said she could not
move her foot, Silvia had hers caught in the

car seatbelt. If one twin was slapped, the other cried, and so on. And then one day, Silvia went to visit her grandparents and Marta stayed home, where she burnt her hand on a hot iron. Her sister, miles away, developed a burn-like sore on the same hand. The wound needed to be dressed by a local doctor. All were in disbelief. The grandparents were adamant that Silvia was not harmed, yet the blister mysteriously appeared.[9]

As if personified in a medieval morality play, Science arrived in the Spanish village in the form of an expert collective: psychologists, psychiatrists and doctors. They launched their formal investigations into Marta and Silvia's relationship. The twins were separated and tested. Marta was taken to one part of the family home, while Silvia was observed for her reactions. One of the investigators performed a short show for Marta with a puppet. Meanwhile, in another part of the house, Silvia was given another puppet to hold. As Marta snatched and threw the puppet, Silvia did the same. Other tests appeared to confirm an interconnectedness between the twins: a light shone into one twin's eyes seemed to cause the other to blink; Marta's patellar reflex was tested by lightly tapping her knees, but Silvia's legs sprang in response; Marta was given perfumes to smell and Silvia held her nose in disgust. The scientists, we are led to understand, left the Landa home baffled. They concluded that younger twins in their home environment might be more likely to connect telepathically.[10] This could be because laboratory tests with adults are rare. And those that are conducted seldom provide such startling results.

On an occasion when psychic and genetic researchers collaborated on the topic, they found that 66 per cent of twins surveyed reported events they judged telepathic in nature.[11] When results were self-reported, monozygotic twins were more likely to experience telepathic events, as were those who also reported that their twin relationship was intimate and their bond strong. Half of all episodes related to the well-being of their co-twin, connected to pain or injury. Unexplained phenomena experienced by twins is an area of research where the interests of twins and the scientific community can diverge; those that gather and analyse data may not collect information about parapsychological events.

The truthfulness of extrasensory perception and twin telepathy confronts scientific orthodoxy in unexpected ways. Australian twins Craig and Brenton Gurney reported being able to feel each other's pain. They have a lifelong connection and a shared catalogue of domestic and sports injuries, serious car accidents and unexplained medical problems that entangle one twin in the other's bad luck. Craig enlisted them in a large twin study that tracked their health over several years. When Craig visited the laboratory, he complained to the researchers that he was experiencing unexplained headaches, but nothing on his brain scans showed anything to be worried about. Weeks later, symptom-free Brenton received scan results that showed a 5-cm (2-in.) tumour at the base of his brain.

In the media reports that followed Brenton's surgery, Western biomedical science and twin magic were treated as sparring partners. Modern twin research had made a timely intervention, alerting doctors to Brenton's unrecognized condition. And when an experimental surgery saved his life, so modern

> ❊❊ June and Jennifer's private conversation sounded more like the twitter of birds than the voices of human children. ❊❊

Marjorie Wallace, *The Silent Twins*, 1986

THE SILENT TWINS MOVIE POSTER
Letitia Wright and Tamara Lawrance star as silent twins June and Jennifer Gibbons in the 2022 movie that recounts the story of their lives.

medicine was celebrated once more. However, researchers and doctors were unable to explain the twins' sympathetic pain, and how or why some twins share these experiences. The twins were 'confounding science'.[12]

The paradox of these twin stories is that they embolden Western scientific materialism and animate alternatives. The validity of parapsychological twin experiences is tested in the domain of science and, in turn, the explanatory power of science can be questioned. Throughout the 19th and 20th centuries efforts were made to give parapsychological research formal recognition and scientific credibility. In London, the Society for Psychical Research was founded in 1882, and other international societies were then established following its model. Throughout the 1920s and 1930s, research institutes at Stanford and Duke universities, and University College London, invested great resources into the formal study of extrasensory perception and a practice called 'psychokinesis', the movement of objects by psychic influence alone. The Parapsychological Association was formed in North Carolina, USA, in 1957 and later affiliated with the American Association for the Advancement of Science. For a time, parapsychic phenomena acquired a measure of popularity. And yet the desire for recognition came with increased scrutiny. Twin studies methods developed in the 1920s and 1930s, which pre-emptively divided environmental and biological factors as well as research subjects based on underlying genetic identities, were then turned towards the parapsychology of twins in the 1970s and 1980s. This led to an emerging consensus that,

despite abundant reported evidence, there was no conclusive proof that twins share a paranormal connection.

Following a research programme backed by the US military in the mid-1980s, the US National Academy of Sciences concluded there was 'no scientific justification from research conducted over a period of 130 years for the existence of parapsychological phenomena'.[13] The same study noted that just 2 per cent of scientists in the National Academy of Sciences believed in parapsychological phenomena or psychic abilities. Scientists that work closely with twins express the same scepticism about strange coincidences, telepathic or extra-sensory connections for twins.[14] By way of explanation, these scientists suggest the biological similarities between pairs of twins raised apart. They point to their upbringings or conditioning, and the intimacy and closeness between some of them. They argue that while twins report such experiences, there is no concrete evidence to prove twins access each other's thoughts or feelings. Twin connections might be guarded by scientists for the risk they pose to a professional monopoly over twins and twinning. Scientific expertise is asserted at the expense of twins and their lived experience, values and beliefs. This puts scientists who work with twins in an uncomfortable position, since they highlight the uncommon power accrued to their profession in recent centuries. ❊❊

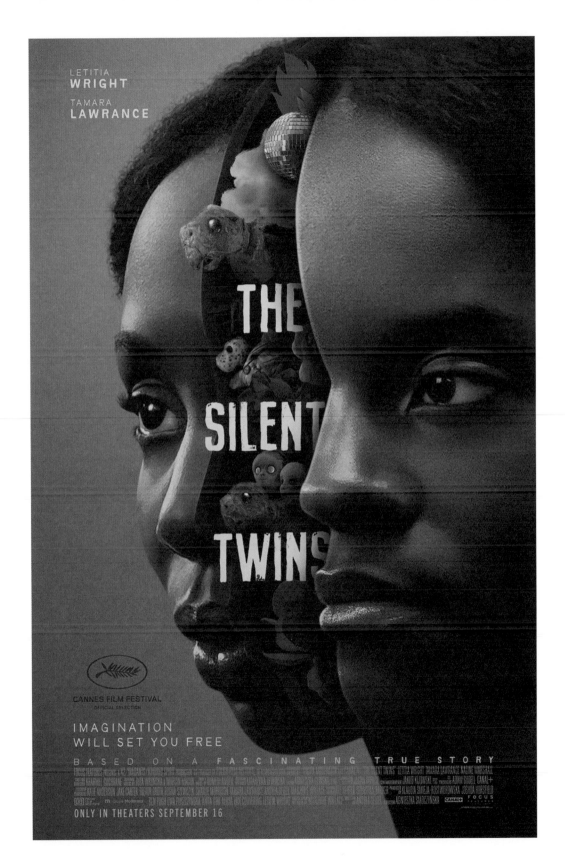

IX.   Twin Communities

━━━━━━━━━━━━━━━━━━━━━━━ ❁ ❁ ━━━━━━━━━━━━━━━━━━━━━━━

Twins are viewed as a community in miniature. They are idealized as intimate relationships that are models for other significant relationships: friendships, romantic pairs, business and creative partnerships. Moreover, they are idealized because they are rare and viewed as desirable. Scientists can be eager to claim it is the genetic make-up of monozygotic twins that means they 'come closer than anyone else to achieving the coordinated, harmonious relations for which we all strive'.[1] But this sense that twins provide a desirable model for Western ideas of harmony and cooperation depends on twins being the exception rather than the rule.

It is not only scientists who are drawn to twins in this way. Psychologists, artists and writers have shown an intense interest in these idealized forms of twin intimacy. Taking one logic to an extreme, French novelist Michel Tournier (1924–2016) imagined the 'geminate world' of twins Jean and Paul in his novel *Les Météores* (1975), picturing a twinship of such physical and emotional closeness that the twins shared 'the same body entwined with its double … entrenched in a mutual rejection of everything outside the other'.[2] Like Shakespeare's twins in *The Comedy of Errors*, who are 'one in semblance', Jean and Paul also offer a countervailing method or way of being, thanks to the familiar backdrop of single-born identity and community.

And yet in some parts of the world, twins are more of a norm than an exception. One such place can be found in Havana, Cuba. In 2013, 68-A Street was home to twelve sets of twins. Locals viewed themselves as a special community that was immune from scientific explanation, where twinship was a strong social tie between and within pairs. They attributed the high number of twins to various factors, including their adherence to a syncretic Afro-Cuban Santería religion, linked to Yoruban twin practices. 'Many say it's the Siguaraya tree, which people ask for things and is in one of the homes,' said Fe Fernandez, one of the street's oldest twins. 'The people believe in it strongly.'[3]

So-called 'twin towns' are places where twinning rates are unusually high. Igbo-Ora in Nigeria has been branded the 'twin capital of the world'. Census data collected in 2013 found that approximately forty-five sets of twins are born per 1,000 live births in a city of 64,431 people.[4] The reasons for higher rates of dizygotic twinning have been studied globally, and they vary according to maternal age, height and diet, as well as a complex set of genetic profiles. However, the exact causes for very local concentrations of twins remain enigmatic. Researchers based at the Lagos University Teaching Hospital hypothesized twin births are linked to a particular diet. Local women eat tuber (yams), which produce the ovary-stimulating hormone phytoestrogen. This remains one hypothesis, so, again, the absence of scientific consensus means local and indigenous knowledges flourish.

In a survey conducted in 2017, Kodinhi in India was estimated to have 400 pairs of twins among a population of 2,000 households,

WALTER AND DAVID OLIVER
These seventy-year-old twins attend the 31st annual Twins Day Festival in Twinsburg, Ohio, in 2006. The event attracts hundreds of twins of all ages every year.

it also is believed to have a twin birth rate of forty-five pairs of twins per 1,000 live births.[5] Located in Kerala's Malappuram district, the town sees rates that continue to grow in ways that confuse scientists, leading researchers to collect saliva, hair samples and other data from twins to seek a molecular explanation. These twin towns present an alternative to twins as minority people, who are not illuminated by clinical, therapeutic and biomedical authorities or feared in a horror tradition that puts groups of twins in villages for the damned. When twins become the norm in exceptional circumstances, there is an opportunity to reflect on the conditions that make them minorities. At these times and in these places, we see for whom twin mirrors are held.

The Twins Days Festival takes place annually in Twinsburg, Ohio. It is a spectacular expression of individual and collective twin identities. The festival is the largest meeting of twins in the world, attracting 2,000 pairs of twins to socialize, take photographs and participate in a wide variety of contests. At the festival's centre is a parade, and 4,000 twins walk through Twinsburg en masse.

Ancient festive traditions of carnival and fete allow temporary suspensions of convention. Anthropologist and twin Dona Lee Davies (b. 1948) spent several years attending Twins Days and other twin events, participating in the carnival rebellion of these occasions. She writes: '... twins play the twin game. They perform or enact the cultural persona of twinship or society's stereotypical caricature of them ... looking as alike as possible is the performance goal of most twin pairs.'[6] The festival creates a rare cultural space where twins satirize expectations and respond to negative stereotypes.

If there is a spirit of rebellion and self-determination at contemporary twin festivals and other gatherings of twins, then the history of psychiatry, psychology, psychoanalysis and psychotherapy has provided plenty of material to work with. Problems emerged in the lives of twin children – indeed, the lives of twins became psychologically concerning – when they were studied by 20th-century psychoanalysts, psychologists and other experts of human behaviour. New stereotypes duly emerged, new fears about the departures twins made from individual norms.

During World War II, US psychoanalyst and partner of Anna Freud (1895–1982) Dorothy Burlingham (1891–1979) set up the first psychoanalytic clinic to treat twins. She believed the progress of twins was constantly endangered and arrested by dependent and competitive relationships. She observed that twins were prone to delinquency and labelled them a 'gang in miniature'.[7] Psychoanalytic models of child development made twins flawed individuals, who failed to pass through a healthy process of individualization. British paediatrician Donald Winnicott (1896–1971) argued it was the conflict and competition over a mother's love that was the cause of twins' 'own particular problems', which he viewed as the 'inherent disadvantage of the twin state'.[8] He reported the regrets of mothers who told him they would have preferred singletons. And he reported twins who told him they would have rather been born alone. By the late 1950s and early 1960s, such views of twins had matured from specialist clinics into orthodoxy.

One important context for Freud and Burlingham's influence on the psychic life of twins is related to the idea of child attachment, which they described and connected to the formation of social relationships and repeating versions of early caregiving patterns into adult life. Later, British psychologist John Bowlby

---

⊜

TWIN GIRLS AT FESTIVAL
Young twin girls prepare to compete for the Most Identical Twin award during the 10th annual Twins Day Festival in Twinsburg, Ohio, in 1985.

❶ FESTIVAL FOUNDING
This 1967 design celebrates 150 years since the founding of Twinsburg and features twin brothers Moses and Aaron Wilcox at its centre.

❷ CARNIVAL ATMOSPHERE
Twins Day festivals draw thousands of participants from all over the world. Twins are encouraged into the playful traditions of carnival.

❸ TWIN COUPLES
Alwin and Lavona Richmond and Lavelda and Arthur Richmond attend the annual convention of the International Twins Association (1990s).

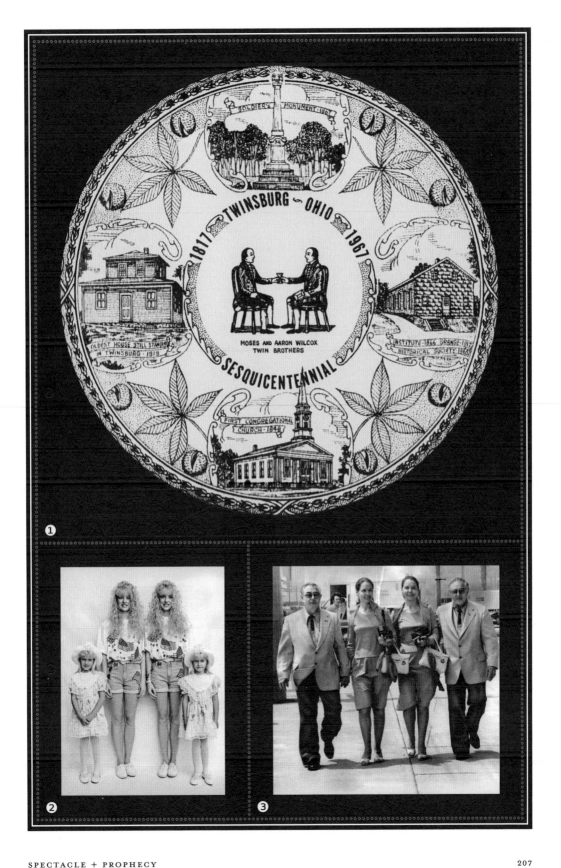

①

②

③

NELSON AND NORBERTO
Photographed in the village of Cândido
Gódoi, Brazil, in 2010 by Noga Shtainer
as part of her *Duo Morality* series.

EVA AND VERONICA
Twins photographed by Noga Shtainer
as part of her *Duo Morality* series (2010).
The village contains an inexplicably
high number of twin births.

LAND OF IBEJI, 2019
A collaborative project by
Bénédicte Kurzen and Sanne
de Wilde, exploring Yoruban
twin beliefs and practices.
'Ibeji' means 'double birth' and
'the inseparable two'. Using
symmetry and resemblance
as tools, the photographers
portray twins as a powerful
metaphor about duality.
According to Yoruban belief,
each human has a spiritual
counterpart. With twins, that
counterpart is physically born.

TWINS DAY TWINS
Eight sets of twins pose at
the 84th annual Twins Day
Festival in Twinsburg, Ohio.
Each twin has chosen to dress
in an identical outfit to their
twin. The festival was held
from 2–4 August 2019.

(1907–90) and US-Canadian developmental psychologist Mary Salter Ainsworth (1913–99) classified attachment into different types or patterns: secure, anxious-ambivalent, disorganized and avoidant.[9] They tried to observe what Ainsworth called the 'strange situation': infants showing distress during separation from their caregivers and relief when reunited. These kinds of distress and relief (or their absence) indicate a style that a person may retain in later life. Such ideas had a profound impact on the psychological and psychotherapeutic treatment of children and adults.[10]

Western children are less likely to be economically active than in previous centuries. Instead, they are viewed as emotionally priceless.[11] In the 1950s and 1960s, psychologists argued twins suffered developmental problems, causing 'mutual identification and part fusion of object and self-representation, leading to a diffusion of ego boundaries between the two individuals.[12] In other words, they feared twins would fail to distinguish themselves from each other. This would jeopardize their social status and their role in the community more generally. Another report from this period gives the example of five-year-old twin girls, observed trying on new dresses. One twin turns to the other: 'Stand over there so I can see how I look.' This interaction was taken as a signal that the little girls risked pathological errors in how they identified with each other. In the language of psychoanalysis, they risked 'serious ego retardation'.[13] Seeing sweetness in the face of your twin or judging one's appearance by another was a source of concern to outsiders.

One doctor, Peter Neubauer (1913–2008), also viewed twins as being threatened, but sought in them a scientific opportunity. He helped set up a now-infamous twin study in New York. Twins were adopted into different families to study the heritability of parental and infant attachment styles. An adoption service separated and placed twin children into different homes, while a scientific team led by Neubauer collected data on twins and triplets. They collaborated to keep adoptive families ignorant: the adoptive families were not told that the children were part of a twin pair. The twins were followed as a cohort until the 1980s, when some parents and twins learnt the truth by chance. These revelations are documented in *The Twinning Reaction* (2017) and *Three Identical Strangers* (2018). The press attention that followed lofted twin research, again, into the controversial limelight,[14] but for decades the study had a murky reputation among twin researchers.[15] Neubauer gave interviews to those who wanted to understand more, but after his death, study documents were sealed and kept secret.[16] When asked why participants were left ignorant about their twin relationships, he explained it was for their own good. He told a former employee and another twin researcher that 'it was "the belief of the time" that being a twin was handicapping'.[17]

The legacies of mid-20th-century twin psychology are still with us. Twins are worried over, treated as singular and discrete units who need to be securely detached from their twin companions and primary caregivers. Western psychologies of twin people are frequently underpinned by a fear of twinship, in which individualism is both prevention and remedy. Twins, parents and

✲✲Give us births, give us male and female, let us deliver two two by two, that we may always hold twin ceremonies here.✲✲

Susan Reynolds Whyte, A common prayer to ancestors in Uganda, 1997

caregivers are instructed in ways that manage twin relationships like they are an accident waiting to happen. The language may have changed, but the thinking remains active among psychologists and therapists, who recommend that twins are dressed differently and are separated at home, school and in other institutions. Twins are also encouraged to have independent friendship groups, interests and a sense of property.[18] Caregivers are asked to manage their fears about twin relationships in these individual terms: they must respond to each recommendation rather than question the power invested in the assumptions, evidence and expertise that counsel them. Meanwhile, utopian pockets of twin creativity and independence are nurtured. These communities suggest hitherto unexplored ways of being twins.

When twins tell others 'I am a twin', it is not only a sibling relationship of which they speak. They reference many changing relationships to each other, to other twins and to the people, places and things that give them meaning, as well as all the ways twins have been used to reveal relations and histories of human culture, biology, technology and political life.

But the history of the human sciences teaches us to make examples of each other. Expert practices such as law, politics, psychology, genetics and the arts encourage the creation of exemplary cases. These hone expertise by knowing, identifying and ranking examples based on their primary relationship to a whole, a group, a population. This style of statistical and algorithmic reasoning puts twins into a series to be computed as figures and examples. They can then be ordered

according to sameness and difference, and made into ideals – attractive, abhorrent – provided they are stripped of the other relationships that are key to their diversity. Made into cases, reformatted as ideal types, they are ready to serve as instruments for powerful cultural practices. The irony of this sleight of hand is that we are made to believe that a community of two form one group, that they are a natural population shaped by a common denominator. And yet, twins are multiple people, existing as part of a diverse and unstable set of populations.

For some readers the pages of this book may confirm the dominant ways of viewing twins: sameness, enduring intimacy and expected cooperation. From these ideals spring a series of contrasting stereotypes about misbehaving evil twins, who may also be uncanny and freakish – physically and psychologically different to all. While it has been impossible to avoid these spectacular values, this book has also shown that behind every twin stereotype stands a set of social, religious, political or economic contexts.

Pick one or a few twins as exemplars, view their history via a partial style of thinking, and then twins are easily tamed and they will go two by two. But one reason that a twin history is difficult to portray in one image or a few hundred, and why this book has approached its work by comparison and thematic collage, is that each twin is what US anthropologist Roy Wagner (1938–2018) might have called a 'fractal person' – neither singular nor plural.[19] If this book has created unexpected journeys, opened avenues that were previously unknown or obscure, then it has realized its purpose. ✲✲

INTRODUCTION (014–029)

1. Mantel, H., 2003, 'Giving up the Ghost', *London Review of Books*, 25 (1).

2. Dickey, R. P., S. N. Taylor *et al*, 2002, 'Spontaneous Reduction of Multiple Pregnancy: Incidence and Effect on Outcome', *American Journal of Obstetric Gynecology*, 186, 77–83; A. Hayto, 2007, *Untwinned: Perspectives on the Death of a Twin Before Birth: An Anthology*. St Albans: Wren.

3. Wright, L., 1997, *Twins: Genes, Environment and the Mystery of Identity*. London: Weidenfeld & Nicolson.

4. Smits, J., and C. Monden, 2011, 'Twinning Across the Developing World', *PLoS One*, 6 (9); C. Monden, G. Pison, and J. Smits, 2021, 'Twin Peaks: More Twinning in Humans Than Ever Before', *Human Reproduction*, 36 (6), 1666–73.

CHAPTER ONE: GODS AND HEROES (032–051)

1. Van Dijk, J., 1995, 'Myth and Mythmaking in Ancient Egypt', in J. M. Sasson (ed.), *Civilizations of the Ancient Near East*. New York: Simon & Schuster; G. Hart, 2005, *The Routledge Dictionary of Egyptian Gods and Goddesses*. London: Routledge; R. H. Wilkinson, 2003, *The Complete Gods and Goddesses of Ancient Egypt*. London: Thames & Hudson.

2. Doniger, W., 2022, 'Wars within the Womb', in K. C. Patton (ed.), *Gemini and the Sacred: Twins and Twinship in Religion and Mythology*. London: Bloomsbury Academic, 213–23.

3. Mallory J. P., and D. Q. Adams, 2006, *The Oxford Introduction to Proto-Indo-European and the Proto-Indo-European World*. Oxford: Oxford University Press; H. J. Walker, 2015, *The Twin Horse Gods: The Dioskouroi in Mythologies of the Ancient World*. London: I. B. Tauris.

4. Apollodorus (trans. R. Hard), 2008, *The Library of Greek Mythology*. Oxford: Oxford University Press.

5. Rutherford, I., 1988, 'Pindar on the Birth of Apollo', *The Classical Quarterly*, 38 (1).

6. Wiseman, T. P., 1995, *Remus: A Roman Myth*. Cambridge: Cambridge University Press; 'Romulus and Remus', *In Our Time*, 24 January 2013. bbc.co.uk/programmes/b01q02t7 Accessed 4 October 2022.

7. Mazzoni, C., 2010, *She-Wolf: The Story of a Roman Icon*. Cambridge: Cambridge University Press.

8. Iverson, P., 2002, *Diné: A History of the Navajos*. New Mexico: University of New Mexico Press.

CHAPTER TWO: EVIL TWINS (052–073)

1. Grim, J., 2022, 'Twins in Native American Mythologies: Relational Transformation', in K. C. Patton(ed.), *Gemini and the Sacred: Twins and Twinship in Religion and Mythology*. London: Bloomsbury Academic, 159.

2. Homer (trans. A. T. Murray), 1924, *Iliad*. Cambridge, MA: Harvard University Press, 602–20.

3. West, M. L. (ed.), 2010, *The Hymns of Zoroaster: A New Translation of the Most Ancient Sacred Texts of Iran*. London: I. B. Tauris.

4. Zaehner, R. C., 1955, *Zurvan: A Zoroastrian Dilemma*. Oxford: Clarendon Press.

5. Guruge, A. W. P. (trans.), 1989, *The Great Chronicle of Sri Lanka*. Colombo: Associated Newspapers of Ceylon; Strathern, A., 2014, 'Vijaya and Romulus: Interpreting the Origin Myths of Sri Lanka and Rome', *Journal of the Royal Asiatic Society*, Series 3, 24 (1), 51–73.

6. Ivarsson, C. H., 2019, 'Lion's Blood: Social Media, Everyday Nationalism and Anti-Muslim Mobilisation among Sinhala-Buddhist Youth', *Contemporary South Asia*, 27 (2), 145–59.

7. Aristotle, 1991, 'The Generation of Animals' in J. Bates (ed.), *The Complete Works of Aristotle: The Revised Oxford Translation*. Princeton, NJ: Princeton University Press, 772a30–772a37.

8. Kudlien, F., 1965, 'The Seven Cells of the Uterus: The Doctrine and its Roots', *Bulletin of the History of Medicine*, 39 (5), 415–23; E. Reichman, 2010, 'Anatomy and the Doctrine of the Seven-Chamber Uterus in Rabbinic Literature', *Hakirah*, 9, 249.

9. Thijssen, J. M., 1987, 'Twins as Monsters: Albertus Magnus's Theory of the Generation of Twins and its Philosophical Context', *Bulletin of the History of Medicine*, 61 (2), 246.

10. Quoted in A. W. Bates, 2005, *Emblematic Monsters: Unnatural Conceptions and Deformed Births in Early Modern Europe*. Amsterdam: Rodopi, 116.

11. Shahar, S., 1990, *Childhood in the Middle Ages*. London: Routledge, 122.

12. Daston, L., and K. Park, 1998, *Wonders and the Order of Nature: 1150–1750*. New York: Zone Books, 57.

13. Bates, A. W., 2002, 'Conjoined Twins in the 16th Century'. *Twin Research*, 5 (6), 521–8; L. Daston, and K. Park, 1998, *Wonders and the Order of Nature: 1150–1750*. New York: Zone Books.

14. Van der Weiden, R., 2004, The First Separation of Conjoined Twins (1689), *Twin Research and Human Genetics*, 7 (2), 125–127.

15. Granzberg, G., 1973, 'Twin Infanticide: A Cross-Cultural Test of a Materialistic Explanation', *Ethos*, 1 (4), 405–12; H. Ball, and C. Hill, 1996, 'Twin Infanticide Revisited', *Current Anthropology*, 37 (5), 856–63; E. A. Pector, 2002 'Twin Death and Mourning Worldwide: A Review of the Literature', *Twin Research*, 5 (3), 196–205.

16. Bastian, M. L., 2001, '"The Demon Superstition": Abominable Twins and Mission Culture in Onitsha History', *Ethnology*, 40 (1), 13–27.

17. Chappel, T. J. H., 1974, 'The Yoruba Cult of Twins in Historical Perspective', *Africa: Journal of the International African Institute*, 44 (3), 250–65.

18. Renne, E. P., 2011, 'The Ambiguous Ordinariness of Yoruba Twins', in P. M. Peek (ed.), *Twins in African and Diaspora Cultures: Double Trouble, Twice Blessed*. Bloomington: Indiana University Press, 307–24.

CHAPTER THREE: TWIN SPIRITS (074–091)

1. Turner, V. [1969], 1997, *The Ritual Process: Structure and Anti-structure*. Piscataway, NJ: Aldine Transaction, 45, 47.

2. Renne, E. P., 2001, 'Twinship in an Ekiti Yoruba Town', *Ethnology*, 40 (1), 63–78.

3. Capone, S., 2011 'Divine Children: The *ibejis* and the *erês* in Brazilian Candomblé', in P. M. Peek (ed.) *Twins in African and Diaspora Cultures. Double Trouble, Twice Blessed*.

Bloomington, IN: Indiana University Press, 290–305.

4. Rich, S. A., 2009, 'The Face of "Lafwa": Vodou & Ancient Figurines Defy Human Destiny', *Journal of Haitian Studies*, 15 (1/2), 262–78; A. M. McGee, 2022, 'Marasa Elou: Twins and Uncanny Children in Haitian Vodou', in K. C. Patton (ed.), *Gemini and the Sacred: Twins and Twinship in Religion and Mythology*. London: Bloomsbury Academic, 127–53.

5. Abe, H. N., 1995, 'From Stereotype to Context: The Study of Japanese Women's Speech', *Feminist Studies*, 21 (3), 657.

6. Belo, J., 1970, *Traditional Balinese Culture*. Columbia, NY: Columbia University Press, 4.

7. Evans-Pritchard, E. E., 1936, 'Customs and Beliefs Relating to Twins Among the Nilotic Nuer', *Uganda Journal*, 3, 234, 236.

8. This was one of E. E., Evans-Pritchard's conclusions, see *Nuer Religion* 1956. Oxford: Clarendon Press, 156.

9. Van Beek W. E. A., and T. Blakely, 1994, 'The Innocent Sorcerer: Coping with Evil in Two African Societies, Kapsiki and Dogon', in W. E. A. Van Beek, T. Blakely, and D. L. Thomson (eds), *African Religion: Experience and Expression*. Oxford: James Currey, 196–228.

10. Royle, N., 2003, *The Uncanny*. Manchester: Manchester University Press, 190.

11. Houlberg, M., 2011, 'Two Equals Three: Twins and the Trickster in Haitian Vodou', in P. M. Peek (ed.), *Twins in African and Diaspora Cultures. Double Trouble, Twice Blessed*. Bloomington, IN: Indiana University Press, 288.

CHAPTER FOUR: NATURE AND NURTURE (094–123)

1. Wright Gillham, N., 2001, *A Life of Sir Francis Galton: From African Exploration to the Birth of Eugenics*. Oxford: Oxford University Press.

2. Galton, F., 1875, 'The History of Twins, as a Criterion of the Relative Powers of Nature and Nurture', *Fraser's Magazine*, 12, 566.

3. Ibid., 574.

4. Freiherr von Verschuer, O., 1939, 'Twin Research from the Time of Francis Galton to the Present-Day', *Proceedings of the Royal Society of London. Series B, Biological Sciences*, 128, 62–81.

5. Weiss, S. F., 2012, 'The Loyal Genetic Doctor, Otmar Freiherr von Verschuer, and the Institut für Erbbiologie und Rassenhygiene: Origins, Controversy, and Racial Political Practice', *Central European History*, 45, 631–68.

6. I discuss the reception of twin studies in more detail in W. Viney, 2016, 'Getting the Measure of Twins' in A. Whitehead, and A. Woods (ed.), *The Edinburgh Companion to the Critical Medical Humanities*. Edinburgh: Edinburgh University Press, 104–119.

7. Chen, E., 1979, 'Twins Reared Apart: A Living Lab', *The New York Times*. nytimes.com/1979/12/09/archives/twins-reared-apart-a-living-lab.html. Accessed 21 October 2022.

8. Tim Spector quoted in L. Jolin, 2013, 'Nature's Control Group', *In Touch*, 22.

9. Segal, N. L., 2017, *Twin Mythconceptions: False Beliefs, Fables, and Facts About Twins*. Cambridge, MA: Academic Press, xxii.

10. Ronald A., R. A. Hoekstra, 2011, 'Autism Spectrum Disorders and Autistic Traits: A Decade of New Twin Studies', *Am J Med Genet Part B*, 156:255–274.

11. Moore, L., T. Le, and G. Fan, 2013, 'DNA Methylation and its Basic Function', *Neuropsychopharmacology*, 38, 23–8. doi. org/10.1038/npp.2012.112.

12. Jonsson, H., E. Magnusdottir *et al*, 2021, 'Differences between Germline Genomes of Monozygotic Twins', *Nature Genetics*, 53 (1), 27–34.

13. Offord, C., 2021, 'Identical Twins Accumulate Genetic Differences in the Womb', *The Scientist*. the-scientist. com/news-opinion/identical-twins-accumulate-genetic-differences-in-the-womb-68324 Accessed 4 October 2022.

14. Joshi, R. S., M. Rigau *et al*, 2022, 'Look-Alike Humans Identified by Facial Recognition Algorithms Show Genetic Similarities', *Cell Reports*, 40 (8).

CHAPTER FIVE: CRIME AND FORENSICS (124–141)

1. 'Madness in the Fast Lane', BBC One. First broadcast 10 August 2010. bbc.co.uk/programmes/b00tf1r4 Accessed 5 October 2022.

2. Quoted in J. McMahon, 2018, 'The Twins Who Ran into Traffic Before Stabbing a Man to Death'. vice.com/en/article/xwpzvj/the-twins-who-ran-into-traffic-before-stabbing-a-man-to-death Accessed 5 October 2022.

3. Chaytor, R., 2009, 'YouTube Motorway Chicken Stabbed Stranger Two Days Later'. mirror.co.uk/news/uk-news/youtube-motorway-chicken-stabbed-stranger-416634 Accessed 5 October 2022.

4. Kray, R., 1993, *My Story*. London: Sidgwick & Jackson, 1.

5. Campbell, D., 2015, 'The Selling of the Krays: How Two Mediocre Criminals Created their Own Legend'. theguardian.com/uk-news/2015/sep/03/the-selling-of-the-krays-how-two-mediocre-criminals-created-their-own-legendlegends Accessed 5 October 2022.

6. Moffitt, T. E., 2005, 'Genetic and Environmental Influences on Antisocial Behaviors: Evidence from Behavioral–Genetic Research', *Advances in Genetics*, 55, 41–104; C. H. Burt, and R. L. Simons, 2014 'Pulling Back the Curtain on Heritability Studies: Biosocial Criminology in the Postgenomic Era', *Criminology: An Interdisciplinary Journal*, 52, 223–62.

7. Ferran, L., 2010, 'Rare Twin Murder Case Echoes Bizarre Fingerprint Origins'. abcnews.go.com/TheLaw/atlanta-twin-murder-case-echoes-fingerprint-origins/story?id=9909586 Accessed 5 October 2022.

8. Rabinow, P., 1993 'Galton's Regret and DNA Typing', *Culture, Medicine and Psychiatry*, 17, 59–65.

9. 'Twin Poachers Mixed Up', *The New York Times*, 2 September 1913. timesmachine.nytimes.com/timesmachine/1913/02/09/100253329.pdf Accessed 5 October 2022.

10. Prosser, D., 2013, 'Like Letting a Fox Guard the Hen House'. hertspastpolicing.org.uk/content/crimes_and_incidents/criminals/the_fox_twins/like_letting_a_fox_guard_the_hen_house Accessed 5 October 2022.

11. Kulish, N., 2009 'Telling Twins Apart Takes New Meaning in Berlin Heist', *The New York Times*. nytimes.

com/2009/02/21/world/europe/21germany.html Accessed 5 October 2022.

12. Biswas, S., K. W. Bowyer, and P. J. Flynn, 2011, 'A Study of Face Recognition of Identical Twins by Humans' in *IEEE International Workshop on Information Forensics and Security*, 1–6.

CHAPTER SIX: BORN AND MADE (142–159)

1. DeVito has multiple epiphyseal dysplasia, otherwise known as Fairbank's disease.

2. Martin, J. A., and M. J. K. Osterman, 2019, 'Is Twin Childbearing on the Decline? Twin Births in the United States, 2014–2018', *NCHS Data Brief*, 351,1–8; R. Cutting, J. Denton, and A. Rutherford, 2011, 'Multiple Births: An Update', *Human Fertility*, 14 (3), 149–50; Association of Clinical Embryologists; Bliss, British Fertility Society, British Infertility Counselling Association, Donor Conception Network, Endometriosis UK, Fertility Friends, Human Fertilisation and Embryology Authority, Infertility Network UK, Miscarriage Association, Multiple Births Foundation, National Gamete Donation Trust, National Perinatal Epidemiology Unit, Royal College of Nursing, Royal College of Obstetricians and Gynaecologists, Royal College of Paediatrics and Child Health, Surrogacy UK, 2011, 'Multiple Births from Fertility Treatment in the UK: A Consensus Statement', *Human Fertility*, 14 (3), 151–3; M. A. Reynolds, L. A. Schieve *et al*, 2003, 'Trends in Multiple Births Conceived Using Assisted Reproductive Technology, United States, 1997–2000', *Pediatrics*, 111 (5), 1159–62; B. Blondel, and M. Kaminski, 2002, 'Trends in the Occurrence, Determinants, and Consequences of Multiple Births', *Seminars in Perinatology*, 26 (4), 239–49.

3. Bowers, N. A. 1998, 'The Multiple Birth Explosion: Implications for Nursing Practice', *Journal of Obstetric, Gynecologic & Neonatal Nursing*, 27 (3), 302–10; R. B. Newman, and B. Luke, 2000, *Multifetal Pregnancy: A Handbook for Care of the Pregnant Patient*. Philadelphia, PA: Lippincott William & Wilkins.

4. Quoted in L. Wright, 1995, 'Double Mystery'. newyorker. com/magazine/1995/08/07/double-mystery Accessed 23 October 2022.

5. Kanter, J. R., S. L. Boulet *et al*, 2015, 'Trends and Correlates of Monozygotic Twinning after Single Embryo Transfer', *Obstetrics and Gynecology*, 125 (1), 111–17.

6. Thernstrom, M., 2010, 'Meet the Twiblings'. nytimes. com/2011/01/02/magazine/02babymaking-t.html Accessed 23 October 2022.

7. Franklin, S., 2013, *Biological Relatives: IVF, Stem Cells, and the Future of Kinship*. Durham, NC: Duke University Press.

8. Inhorn, M. C., 2015, *Cosmopolitan Conceptions: IVF Sojourns in Global Dubai*. Durham, NC: Duke University Press; A. Hodegkiss, and E. Innes, 2013, 'British Couple to Become Parents of TWO Sets of Surrogate Twin Babies Carried by Women in India', *MailOnline*, 2013, dailymail. co.uk/health/article-2478233/British-couple-parents-TWO-sets-surrogate-twin-babies-carried-women-India.html Accessed 23 October 2022.

9. Inhorn, M. C., P. Shrivastav, and P. Patrizio, 2012, 'Assisted Reproductive Technologies and Fertility "Tourism":

Examples from Global Dubai and the Ivy League', *Medical Anthropology*, 31:3, 249–265.

10. Maria del Carmen Bousada, quoted in 'Woman Who Had Twins at 66 Dies', *The Guardian*. theguardian.com/ lifeandstyle/2009/jul/15/bousada-oldest-new-mother-dies Accessed 22 October 2022.

11. Georgiadis, K, 2011, '"Octomum" Doctor's Medical Licence Revoked'. progress.org.uk/octomum-doctors-medical-licence-revoked/Accessed 23 October 2022.

12. Martin, J. A., and M. J. K. Osterman, 2019, 'Is Twin Childbearing on the Decline? Twin Births in the United States, 2014–2018'.

13. The President's Council on Bioethics 2002 *Human Cloning and Human Dignity: An Ethical Enquiry*. Washington D.C. PCBE, 103.

CHAPTER SEVEN: BORN ENTERTAINERS (162–191)

1. Poe, E. A., 1939, *The Fall of the House of Usher*.

2. Orser, J. A., 2014, *The Lives of Chang & Eng: Siam's Twins in Nineteenth-Century America*. University of North Carolina Press.

3. Domurat Dreger, A., 2004, *One of Us: Conjoined Twins and the Future of Normal*. Cambridge, MA: Harvard University Press, 22–9.

4. Anonymous, quoted in S. O'Donnell, 2020, "Boys will be.... – The Rocky Twins" godsandfoolishgrandeur.blogspot.com/ 2020/09/the-rocky-twins.html Accessed 19 November 2022.

5. Schwartz, H., 1996, *The Culture of the Copy: Striking Likenesses, Unreasonable Facsimiles*. Cambridge, MA: Zone Books.

6. Quoted in P. Farmer, 1996, *Two, or: The Book of Twins and Doubles*. London: Virago, 182.

7. Ngai, S., 2015, *Our Aesthetic Categories: Zany, Cute, Interesting*. Cambridge, MA: Harvard University Press.

CHAPTER EIGHT: TWINS AND THE PARANORMAL (192–201)

1. Reported in I. Stevenson, 1970 *Telepathic Impressions*. Charlottesville: University Press of Virginia.

2. Bingham, J., 2009, 'Twin's "Sixth Sense" Saves Drowning Sister', *The Telegraph*. telegraph.co.uk/news/ uknews/5036835/Twins-sixth-sense-saves-drowning-sister. html Accessed 21 October 2022.

3. Wesley, J., 1830, 'Murder Prevented by a Threefold Dream', *The Works of the Rev. John Wesley A.M.* London: John Mason, 496.

4. Farah, M., 2013, *Twin Ambitions*. London: Hodder & Stoughton, 1.

5. The campaign for justice was led by Marjorie Wallace, whose advocacy inspired many newspaper articles, theatre and film adaptations. See M. Wallace, 1993, *The Silent Twins* Penguin: London.

6. Stevenson. I., cited in K. M. Wehrstein, 2017, 'Twin Reincarnation Research', *Psi Encyclopedia*. London: The Society for Psychical Research https://psi-encyclopedia.spr.ac.uk/articles/twins-reincarnation-research Accessed 28 February, 2023.

7. Jamison, T., and L. Jamison, 2011, *Psychic Intelligence: Tune in and Discover the Power of Your Intuition*. New York: Grand Central Life & Style.

8. Yahoo News 2011 'How Psychic Twins Predicted 9/11 Terrorist Attacks', au.news.yahoo.com/how-psychic-twins-predicted-9-11-terrorist-attacks-9878867.html#page1 Accessed 21 October 2022.

9. Dossey, L., 2018, 'The One Mind', *Tikkun*, 33 (4), 41–8.

10. The story of Marta and Silvia is also recalled in G. L. Playfair, 2002, *Twin Telepathy: The Psychic Connection*. London: Vega Books.

11. Brusewitz, G, L. Cherkas *et al*, 2013, 'Exceptional Experiences Amongst Twins', *Journal of the Society for Psychical Research*, 77 (913), 220–35.

12. Signy, H., 'Twin Power: The Supernatural Siblings Confounding Science'. rdasia.com/true-stories-lifestyle/twin-power-supernatural-siblings-confounding-science Accessed 12 October 2022.

13. National Research Council, 1988, *Enhancing Human Performance: Issues, Theories, and Techniques*. Washington, D.C.: The National Academies Press, 22.

14. Segal, N. L., 2017, *Twin Mythconceptions*. San Diego, CA: Academic Press, 143–61.

CHAPTER NINE: TWIN COMMUNITIES (202–215)

1. Segal, N. L., 1999, *Entwined Lives: Twins and What They Tell Us About Human Behavior*. New York: Putnam, 101. Scientists have been interested in showing how twins are more or less intimate than singletons. See I. Petersen, T. Martinussen *et al*, 2011, 'Lower Marriage and Divorce Rates Among Twins than Among Singletons in Danish Birth Cohorts 1940–1964', *Twin Research and Human Genetics*, 14, 150–7; C. M. Tancredy, and R. C. Fraley, 2006 'The Nature of Adult Twin Relationships: An Attachment-Theoretical Perspective', *Journal of Personality and Social Psychology*, 90 (1), 78–93.

2. Tournier, M. (trans. A. L. Carter), 1981, *Gemini*. London: Collins, 330, 11–12.

3. Quoted in Associated Press, 2013, 'Havana Street Produces 12 Sets of Twins'. theguardian.com/world/2013/oct/04/havana-street-12-sets-twins Accessed 24 October 2022.

4. Omonkhua, A. A., F. E. Okonofua *et al*, 2020, 'Community Perceptions on Causes of High Dizygotic Twinning Rate in Igbo-Ora, South-West Nigeria: A Qualitative Study', *PLoS ONE*, 15 (12), e0243169.

5. Wilson, C., 2019, 'An Indian Village Has Many More Twins Than Can Be Explained', *The New Scientist*. newscientist.com/article/2201023-an-indian-village-has-many-more-twins-than-can-be-explained/ Accessed 24 October 2022.

6. Davis, D. L., 2014, *Twins Talk: What Twins Tell Us About Person, Self, and Society*. Athens, OH: Ohio University Press, 62–3.

7. Burlingham, D., 1949, 'Twins: A Gang in Miniature' in K. R. Eissler (ed.), *Searchlights on Delinquency: New Psychoanalytic Studies Dedicated to Professor August Aichhorn on the Occasion of his Seventieth Birthday, July 27, 1948*. New York: International Universities Press.

8. Winnicott, D. W., 2016, 'Twins' in L. Caldwell, and H. T. Robinson (eds), *The Collected Works of D. W. Winnicott: Volume 2, 1939–1945*. New York: online edition, Oxford Academic. https://doi.org/10.1093/med:psych/9780190271343.003.0055 Accessed 14 November 2022.

9. Bowlby, J., 1969, *Attachment and Loss: Vol 1*. New York: Basic Books; Salter Ainsworth, M D, 1991 'Attachments and Other Affectional Bonds Across the Life Cycle', in C. M. Parkes, J. Stevenson-Hinde and P. Marris (eds), *Attachment Across the Lifecycle*. New York: Routledge, 33–51.

10. Attachment theory reflects Western middle-class family values and care models. Parenting is assumed to come in families that are small, nuclear and contained in households of two generations. Attachment patterns assume mothers have children one at a time and attachment is a biographical dynamic created from one or two adults, and one child. *See also* R. Duschinsky, 2020, *Cornerstones of Attachment Research*. Oxford: Oxford University Press; H. Keller, 2018, 'Universality Claim of Attachment Theory: Children's Socioemotional Development Across Cultures', *Proceedings of the National Academy of Sciences*, 115 (45), 11414–19; C. R. Fraley, and C. M. Tancredy, 2012, 'Twin and Sibling Attachment in a Nationally Representative Sample', *Personality and Social Psychology Bulletin*, 38 (3), 308–16.

11. The phrase is adapted from C. Steedman, 1995, *Strange Dislocations: Childhood and the Idea of Human Interiority, 1780–1930*. London: Virago.

12. Joseph, E. D., and J. H. Tabor, 1961, 'The Simultaneous Analysis of a Pair of Identical Twins and the Twinning Reaction', *The Psychoanalytic Study of the Child*, 16 (1), 275–99.

13. Leonard, M. R., 1961, 'Problems in Identification and Ego Development in Twins', *The Psychoanalytic Study of the Child*, 16 (1), 300–20.

14. *Three Identical Strangers*, 2018. USA: CNN Films, RAW; *The Twinning Reaction*, 2017. USA: Fire Horse Films.

15. For example, see L. Wright, 1995, 'Double Mystery', *The New Yorker*. newyorker.com/magazine/1995/08/07/double-mystery Accessed 24 October 2022.

16. Perlman, L. M., and N. L. Segal, 2005, 'Memories of the Child Development Center Study of Adopted Monozygotic Twins Reared Apart: An Unfulfilled Promise', *Twin Research and Human Genetics: The Official Journal of the International Society for Twin Studies*, 8 (3), 271–81.

17. Ibid., 274.

18. For an example of this advice, see B. Klein, 2021, 'Raising Twins to Be Individuals and Trusted Friends'. psychologytoday.com/gb/blog/twin-dilemmas/202103/raising-twins-be-individuals-and-trusted-friends Accessed 24 October 2022.

19. Wagner, R., 1991, 'The Fractal Person' in M. Godelier, and M. Strathern (eds), *Big Men and Great Men: Personifications of Power in Melanesia*. Cambridge: Cambridge University Press, 162.

Daston, L., and K. Park, 1998, *Wonders and the Orders of Nature: 1150–1750*. New York: Zone Books.

Dostoevsky, F. [1846], (trans. E. Harden), 1985, *The Double: Two Versions*. Ann Arbor: Ardis, 132.

Doyle, A. C. [1892], 1965, *The Adventure of the Speckled Band and Other Stories of Sherlock Holmes*. New York: The New American Library, Inc., 22.

Hesiod [c. 700–730 BC], (trans D. Hine), 2005, 'Theogony', *Works of Hesiod and the Homeric Hymns*. Chicago & London: The University of Chicago Press, 84.

Irwin, H. J., and C. A. Watt, 2007, *An Introduction to Parapsychology*, 5th edn. North Carolina: McFarland & Company, Inc., Publishers, 209.

Lash, J., 1993, *Twins and the Double*. London: Thames & Hudson, 78.

Pearson, J. [1972], 2015, *The Profession of Violence: The Rise and Fall of the Kray Twins*. London: William Collins, 9.

Scheinfeld, A., 1967, *Twins and Supertwins*. Philadelphia and New York: J. B. Lippincott Company, 36.

Schwartz, H., 1996, *The Culture of the Copy: Striking Likenesses, Unreasonable Facsimiles*. New york: Zone Books, 7, 51.

Selasi, T., 2022, 'Betwixt and Betwin', *Granta*, 161, 119.

Wallace, M. [1986], 1987, *The Silent Twins*. New York: Ballantine Books, 36.

Whyte, S. R., 1997, 'A common prayer to ancestors in Eastern Uganda', *Questioning Misfortune*. Cambridge: Cambridge University Press, 55.

FURTHER READING

Ball, H., and C. Hill, c.1996, 'Re-evaluating Twin Infanticide', *Current Anthropology*, 37 (5), 856–63.

Ball, L. C., and T. Teo, 'Twin Studies' in W. A. Darity, 2008, *The International Encyclopaedia of Social Sciences*, 2nd edn, New York: Palgrave, 473–5.

Chappel, T. J. H., 1974, 'The Yoruba Cult of Twins in Historical Perspective', *Africa: Journal of the International African Institute*, 44 (3), 250–65.

Chatwin, B., 1982, *On Black Hill*. London: Jonathan Cape.

Dasen, V., 2005, *Jumeaux, Jumelles dans l'Antiquite grecque et romaine*. Zurich: Akanthus.

Daston, L., and K. Park, 1998, *Wonders and the Order of Nature: 1150–1750*. New York: Zone Books.

Davis, D. L., 2014, *Twins Talk: What Twins Tell Us about Person, Self, and Society*. Athens: Ohio University Press.

De Nooy, J., 2005, *Twins in Contemporary Literature and Culture: Look Twice* Basingstoke: Palgrave.

Diduk, S., 2001, 'Twinship and Juvenile Power: The Ordinariness of the Extraordinary', *Ethnology*, 40 (1), 29–43.

Dreger, A. D., 2004, *One of Us: Conjoined Twins and the Future of Normal*. Cambridge, MA: Harvard University Press.

Farmer, P., 1996, *Two, or The Book of Twins and Doubles: An Autobiographical Anthology*. London: Virago.

Franklin, S., 2013, *Biological Relatives: IVF, Stem Cells, and the Future of Kinship*. Durham, NC: Duke University Press.

Galton, F., 1875, 'The History of Twins as a Criterion of Nature and Nurture', *Fraser's Magazine*, 12, 566–76.

Gross, K., 2003, 'Ordinary Twinship', *Raritan*, 22 (4), 20–39.

Hacking, I., 2007, 'Kinds of People: Moving Targets', *Proceedings of the British Academy*, 151, 285–318.

Hall, J., 2003, 'Twinning', *The Lancet*, 362, 735–43.

Kristóf, Á. (trans. A. Sheridan), 1997, *The Notebook, The Proof, The Third Lie: Three Novels* New York: Grove.

King, E., 2022, *Twins and Recursion in Digital, Literary and Visual Cultures*. London: Bloomsbury Academic.

Lykken, D. T., 1982, 'Research with Twins: The Concept of Emergenesis', *Psychophysiology*, 19, 361–373.

Patton, K. C. (ed), 2022, *Gemini and the Sacred: Twins and Twinship in Religion and Mythology*. London: Bloomsbury Academic.

Peek, P. M. (ed), 2011, *Twins in African and Diaspora Cultures: Double Trouble, Twice Blessed*. Bloomington, IN: Indiana University Press.

Selasi, T., 2022, 'Betwixt and Betwin', *Granta* 161, 114–127.

Schwartz, H., 1996, *The Culture of the Copy: Striking Likenesses, Unreasonable Facsimiles*. Cambridge MA: Zone.

Seabrook, J., 2006 'Twins', *Granta* 95, 191–207.

Segal, N. L., 2012, *Born Together – Reared Apart: The Landmark Minnesota Twin Study*. Cambridge, MA: Harvard University Press.
— 2017 *Twin Mythconceptions: False Beliefs, Fables, and Facts about Twins*. San Diego, CA: Academic Press.

Teo, T., and L. C. Ball, 2009, 'Twin Research, Revisionism and Metahistory', *History of the Human Sciences*, 22 (5), 1–23.

Tellegan A., D. T. Lykken, T. J. Bouchard, K. Wilcox, S. Rich, N. L. Segal, 1988, 'Personality Similarity in Twins Reared Apart and Together', *Journal of Personality and Social Psychology*, 54, 1031–1039.

Thijssen, J. M., 1987, 'Twins as Monsters: Albertus Magnus's Theory of the Generation of Twins and its Philosophical Context', *Bulletin of the History of Medicine*, 61 (2), 237–46.

Thompson, R. F., 1971, 'Sons of Thunder: Twin Images among the Oyo and Other Yoruba Groups', *African Arts*, 4 (3), 8–80.

Tournier, M. (trans. A. L. Carter), 1981, *Gemini*. London: Collins Books.

Turner, V. [1969], 1997, *The Ritual Process: Structure and Anti-structure*. Piscataway, NJ: Transaction Publishers.

Viney W., 2021, *Twins: Superstitions and Marvels, Fantasies and Experiments*. London: Reaktion Books.

Zazzo, R., 1984, *Le Paradoxe des jumeaux: précédé d'un dialogue avec Michel Tournier*. Paris: Stock-Laurence Pernoud.

SOURCES OF ILLUSTRATIONS
SOURCES OF ILLUSTRATIONS

Every effort has been made to locate and credit copyright holders of the material reproduced in this book. The author and publisher apologize for any omissions or errors, which can be corrected in future editions.

a=above, **b**=below, **c**=centre, **l**=left, **r**=right

2 Rumsey Collection; **4–5** Tate, London. Photo Album/Alamy Stock Photo; **6–7** Photo Carol M. Highsmith. Library of Congress Prints and Photographs Division, Washington, D.C. (LC-HS503- 6412); **8–9** Photo Matthew J. Cotter; **10** Wellcome Collection, London; **12** Photo Camilla Jessel; **14** Rijksmuseum, Amsterdam (SK-A-981); **16** Drew University Library, Madison NJ; **17** Bibliothèque interuniversitaire de santé, Paris; **19a** Library of Congress Prints and Photographs Division, Washington, D.C. (LC-DIG-nclc-02616); **19b** Library of Congress Prints and Photographs Division, Washington, D.C. (LC-DIG-nclc-03240); **20** Private collection; **22, 23** University of California Libraries; **25a** Mumok (Museum moderner Kunst Stiftung Ludwig Wien). Schenkung Joachim Diederichs/donation by Joachim Diederichs 2007 (MD 163/0). Richard Kriesche © DACS 2023; **25b** Neue Galerie Graz, Universalmuseum Joanneum. Richard Kriesche © DACS 2023; **26** © Noga Shtainer; **28–29** Photo Visual China Group via Getty Images; **30** DK Images/Science Photo Library; **32** Metropolitan Museum of Art, New York. Rogers Fund, 1930 (30.4.142); **34** Photo Fine Art Images/Heritage Images/Getty Images; **35** Palazzo Pitti, Gallery of Modern Art, Florence. Photo Scala, Florence – courtesy of the Ministero Beni e Att. Culturali e del Turismo; **36a** The Trustees of the British Museum, London; **36cl** Metropolitan Museum of Art, New York. Gift of Egyptian Exploration Fund, 1896 (96.4.4) **36cr** Photo Album/Alamy Stock Photo; **36bl** Photo Artokoloro/Alamy Stock Photo; **36br** Metropolitan Museum of Art, New York. Fletcher Fund, 1963 (63.152); **38–39** Photo The Picture Art Collection/Alamy Stock Photo; **40** Los Angeles County Museum. From the Nasli and Alice Heeramaneck Collection, Museum Associates Purchase (M.83.1.7); **42–43** Wellcome Collection, London; **44** Royal Collection, London (RCIN 407294); **46** Leeds City Museum; **47** Mondadori Portfolio/Archivio Lensini/Fabio e Andrea Lensini/Bridgeman Images; **49al** Photo Peter Horree/Alamy Stock Photo; **49ac, 49ar** Photo Werner Forman/Universal Images Group/Getty Images; **49c** Photo agefotostock/Alamy Stock Photo; **49bl** Los Angeles County Museum. Purchased with funds provided by Camilla Chandler Frost (M.2010.115.409); **49br** Photo Dankger/Dreamstine.com; **50, 51** British Library Board. All Rights Reserved/Bridgeman Images; **52** darkbird77/iStock; **54a** House of the Vettii, Pompeii; **54b** Alexandros A. Lavdas/Shutterstock; **56** Bibliothèque nationale de France, Paris (Lat. 16169, fol. 134r); **57** Bodleian Library, Oxford (MS. Bodl. 264); **58** A. Dagli Orti/NPL – DeA Picture Library/Bridgeman Images; **59** Museo Provinciale Campano, Capua, Italy. Photo DeAgostini Picture Library/Scala, Florence; **60al** British Library, London (MS Royal 15 E VI fol. 273r); **60ar** Bibliothèque nationale de l'Arsenal, Paris, MS 5077 f.82); **60c** The Picture Art Collection/Alamy Stock Photo; **60bl** Bibliothèque Sainte-Geneviève, Paris, France. Photo Archives Charmet/Bridgeman Images; **60br** Museo dell'Accademia dei Concordi, Rovigo, Italy. Photo Luisa Ricciarini/Bridgeman Images; **62–63** Dordrechts Museum, Netherlands; **64, 65** McGill University Library, Toronto; **67–71** Wellcome Collection, London; **72–73** Library of Congress Prints and Photographs Division, Washington, D.C. (LC-B2- 2526-11 [P&P]); **74** Metropolitan Museum of Art, New York. The Michael C. Rockefeller Memorial Collection, Bequest of Nelson A. Rockefeller, 1979 (1979.206.294). Digital image The Metropolitan Museum of Art/Art Resource/Scala, Florence; **76–77** Wellcome Collection, London; **79al** Metropolitan Museum of Art, New York. Gift of Mr. and Mrs. Klaus G. Perls, 1991 (1991.17.138); **79ar** Saint Louis Art Museum, Missouri, Photo Saint Louis Art Museum/Museum Shop Fund/Bridgeman Images; **79cr** Metropolitan Museum of Art, New York. Gift of Meredith Howland, 1904 (04.34.8); **79bl** Museum of Anatolian Civilisations, Ankara, Turkey. Photo Tarker/Bridgeman Images; **79br** Musée du quai Branly – Jacques Chirac, Paris. Photo musée du quai Branly – Jacques Chirac, Dist. RMN-Grand Palais/Claude Germain; **80** Fitzwilliam Museum, University of Cambridge/Bridgeman Images; **82** Photo Lee Moorhouse. Library of Congress Prints and Photographs Division, Washington, D.C. (LC-DIG-ds-12821); **83** Photo Lee Moorhouse. Library of Congress Prints and Photographs Division, Washington, D. C. (LC-DIG-ds-12822); **85al** Metropolitan Museum of Art, New York. Gift of F. Peter Rose, 1981 (1981.424.7). Digital image The Metropolitan Museum of Art/Art Resource/Scala, Florence; **85ac** The Art Institute of Chicago. Gift of Deborah Stokes and Jeffrey Hammer (1982.1513–14). Digital image The Art Institute of Chicago/Art Resource, NY/Scala, Florence; **85ar** National Museum, Lagos, Nigeria. Photo akg-images/André Held; **85b** Musée du quai Branly – Jacques Chirac, Paris. Photo RMN-Grand Palais (musée du quai Branly – Jacques Chirac)/Daniel Arnaudet; **86–87** Musée du quai Branly – Jacques Chirac, Paris. Musée du quai Branly – Jacques Chirac, Dist. RMN-Grand Palais/Claude Germain; **88** Bodleian Library, Oxford (MS. Bodl. Or. 133); **89** Georgian State Picture Gallery, Tbilisi, Georgia/Bridgeman Images; **90–91** Bodleian Library, Oxford (MS. Bodl. Or. 133); **92** Simon Fraser/Science Photo Library; **94** Wellcome Collection, London; **96, 97** Courtesy Sara Ozvaldic at Barnbrook; **98a** Courtesy Eldersveld, Reddit.com; **98b** Courtesy Tomasz Dziedzic, previously pulished in Dziedzic, Tomasz & Fabiańska, Ewa & Toeplitz, Zuzanna, *Handwriting of Monozygotic and Dizygotic Twins. Problems of Forensic Sciences*, 69. 30–36 (2007); **100–101** The Harry H. Laughlin Papers, Truman State University, photograph, Blk Photo 2, 38; **102, 103** University of Florida, George A. Smathers Libraries; **104, 105** Archives of the Max Planck Society, Berlin; **107al, 107ar** United States Holocaust Memorial Museum, courtesy of Yehudit Csengri Barnea; **107c** United States Holocaust Memorial Museum, courtesy of Belarusian State Archive of Documentary Film and Photography; **107bl** United States Holocaust Memorial Museum collection, gift of Yehudit Barnea and Lea Huber; **107br** United States Holocaust Memorial Museum, courtesy of Irene Guttmann Slotkin Hizme; **109–111** University of Florida, George A. Smathers Libraries; **112al, 112ar, 112bl** Photo Thomas J Bouchard Jr. Photograph taken in David Lykken's laboratory, previously published in *Born Together-Reared part: The Landmark Minnesota Twin Study*, by Nancy L. Segal (Harvard University Press, 2012); **112c** CineMaterial.com; **112br** Photo Nancy L. Segal. Photograph taken in Los Angeles as the twins headed home from Minneapolis, previously published in *Born Together-Reared part: The Landmark Minnesota Twin Study*, by Nancy L. Segal (Harvard University Press, 2012); **114a** Published in *Twins Reared Together and Apart: The Science Behind the Fascination*, by Nancy L. Segal (2017) https://www.amphilsoc.org/sites/default/files/2017-07/attachments/Segal.pdf; **114b** Data adapted from Lykken, 'Research with Twins: The Concept of Emergenesis,' *Psychophysiology* 19 (1982): 361 – 373. From *Born Together-Reared part: The Landmark Minnesota Twin Study*, by Nancy L. Segal (Harvard University Press, 2012); **115a** Data adapted from Tellegan et al. 'Personality Similarity in Twins Reared Apart and Together', Journal of Personality and Social Psychology 54, (1988): 1031–1039. From *Born Together-Reared part: The Landmark Minnesota Twin Study*, by Nancy L. Segal (Harvard University Press, 2012); **115b** Data adapted from Lykken, 'Research with Twins: The Concept of Emergenesis,' *Psychophysiology* 19 (1982): 361 – 373. From *Born Together-Reared part: The Landmark Minnesota Twin Study*, by Nancy L. Segal (Harvard University Press, 2012); **117a** Photo Lisa Wiltse/Corbis via Getty Images; **117b** Photo © Robin Nelson. ZUMA Press, Inc./Alamy Stock Photo; **118–119** Photo Twins Days, Inc.; **121** from *I'm Not A Look-Alike!* by François Brunelle; **122** NASA; **124** Wellcome Collection, London; **126** Bibliomediateca Mario Gromo del Museo nazionale del cinema, Turin; **127** Wellcome Collection, London; **129** Photo Popperfoto via Getty Images/Getty Images; **130a** Photo Evening Standard/Hulton Archive/Getty Images; **130b** Photo Keystone/Getty Images; **131a** Photo Larry Ellis/Express/Getty Images; **131b** Photo Express Newspapers/Getty Images; **132al, 132ar, 132c** Courtesy of 'The History of Fingerprints' article, https://onin.com/fp/fphistory.html; **132b** North Hertfordshire Museum, Hitchin; **134–135** Library of Congress Prints and Photographs Division, Washington, D.C.; **136, 137** Francis A. Countway Library of Medicine, Harvard University; **138a, 138b** Photo Los Angeles Examiner/USC/Libraries/Corbis via GettyImages; **140al, 140acl** © 2023 Oxygen Media, LLC. A Division of NBCUniversal; **140ar** Photo Bruce C. Strong/MediaNews Group/Orange County Register via Getty Images; **140acr** Photo Paul E. Rodriquez/MediaNews Group/Orange County Register via Getty Images; **140bcl** *People* magazine, February 2, 2018; **140bl** Mike Groll/AP/Shutterstock; **140bcr, 140br** Photo Darrell Everidge/ Covington News; **142** Sebastian Kaulitzki/Science Photo Library; **144, 145** CineMaterial.com; **146** Photo BSIP/Universal Images group via Getty Images; **148a** Photo Antonio Faccilongo/Getty Images Reportage; **148b** Photo Jean-Francois Monier/AFP via Getty Images; **150–151** Photo Sebastien Micke/Paris Match/Contour by Getty Images; **153a** Photo Brent N. Clarke/Getty Images; **153b** Photo Richard Heathcote/Getty Images; **154** Data adapted from 'Twin Peaks: more twinning in humans than ever before', *Human Reproduction*, Volume 36, Issue 6, June 2021, 1666–1673; **155a** Qwerty/Alamy Stock Photo; **155b** Martin Shields/Alamy Stock Photo; **157** Photo Robin Hammond/Panos Pictures **158a** Photo Colin McPherson/Corbis via Getty Images **158b** Photo Michael Smith/Hulton Archive via Getty Images; **159a** Reuters/Alamy Stock Photo; **159b** Wenn Rights Ltd/Alamy Stock Photo; **160** Photo Buyenlarge/Getty Images; **162** Prismatic Pictures/Bridgeman Images; **164a, 164b** Library of Congress Prints and Photographs Division, Washington, D.C. ; **165a, 165b** New York Public Library; **166ar, 166al** Illustration by William Hatherell for *The Prince and the Pauper* by Mark Twain (Harper & Brothers Publishers, 1909); **166bl, 166br** Illustrations by Byam Shaw for *Selected Tales of Mystery* by Edgar Allan Poe (Sidgwick & Jackson, 1909); **168** Illustration by Harry Clarke for 'William Wilson', *Tales of Mystery and Imagination* by Edgar Allan Poe. (G. G. Harrup, 1923); **169** AF Fotografie/Alamy Stock Photo; **170–173** Wellcome Collection, London; **175** Photo Heritage Art/Heritage Images via Getty Images; **176** Photo Margaret Chute/Getty Images; **177** Photo Hulton Archive/Getty Images; **178–179** Private collection; **180a, 180b** Everett Collection Inc./Alamy Stock Photo; **181a** Glasshouse Images/Shutterstock; **181b** Everett Collection Inc./Alamy Stock Photo; **182–183** CineMaterial.com; **184a** AJ Pics/Alamy Stock Photo; **184b** Marka/Alamy Stock Photo; **185a** TCD/Prod.DB/Alamy Stock Photo; **185b** Collection Christophel/Alamy Stock Photo; **187a** Photo ABC Photo Archives/Disney General Entertainment Content via Getty Images; **187b** TCD/Prod.DB/Alamy Stock Photo; **188al** Photo Daniele Venturelli/Getty Images for Gucci; **190–191** Photo © Matteo Canestraro; **192** Photo Wilton Montenegro. Image licensed by the Tunga Institute. © Instituto Tunga; Courtesy of Instituto Tunga, Rio de Janiero and Luhring Augustine, New York; **194** © Roger Ballen; **195** Photo © Andrej Glusgold, *After Hitchcock*, 2000; **196** Photo Joe Tamel. Courtesy The Psychic Twins; **199** Trinity Mirror/Mirrorpix/Alamy Stock Photo; **201** CineMaterial.com; **202** Photo J.D. Pooley/Getty Images; **204–205** Bettmann/Getty Images; **207a** Private collection; **207bl** Photo Evan Hurd/Corbis via Getty Images; **207br** Photo Jeff Goode/Toronto Star via Getty Images; **208, 209** © Noga Shtainer; **210a, 210b** Courtesy Bénédicte Kurzen and Sanne de Wilde; **212–213** Photo Josie Gealer/Getty Images; **215** Photo Visual China Group via Getty Images

ACKNOWLEDGMENTS
ACKNOWLEDGMENTS

ABOUT THE AUTHOR
ABOUT THE AUTHOR

❋ ❋

Many people have helped me professionally and personally. I'm very grateful to friends and colleagues at the universities of Durham, Goldsmiths and Imperial College London who let me learn from their experience and expertise. And to a wider community of twins and twin researchers who have encouraged my research. Thank you to the Leverhulme Trust and Wellcome Trust for their financial support. Thank you, too, for the skill and patience of Jane Laing, Tristan de Lancey, Georgina Kyriacou, Sadie Butler, Becky Gee and Phoebe Lindsley at Thames & Hudson. And to the two reviewers who provided their feedback on the manuscript, thank you. This book is dedicated to twins and to those who care for them.

William Viney is a health researcher who has worked at Durham University, Goldsmiths, University of London and Imperial College London. His writing has appeared in *Cabinet Magazine*, *Critical Quarterly*, *Frieze* and the *Times Literary Supplement*. He is the author of *Waste: A Philosophy of Things* (2014) and *Twins: Superstitions and Marvels, Fantasies and Experiments* (2021). In 2017 he directed a documentary short, *Twins on Twins*.

❋ ❋

PAGE 2
CASTOR AND POLLUX FORM GEMINI
Astronomical print of the Gemini twins by A. Jamieson (1822). The 'Heavenly Twins' spend their days in Hades and nights on Mount Olympus, the 'sky's golden palaces'.

PAGES 4—5
CHOLMONDELEY LADIES, C. 1600—10
Oil painting of two young women sitting up in bed, each cradling an infant. The inscription at the base of the painting states: 'Two ladies of the Cholmondeley Family, Who were born the same day, Married the same day, And brought to Bed [gave birth] the same day'.

PAGES 6—7
MARIAN AND VIVIAN BROWN
The twins enjoy afternoon tea in the 1990s. They were neighbourhood celebrities in San Francisco. Often seen together and dressed alike, they regularly appeared in television advertisements.

PAGES 8—9
THE GRADY TWINS COSTUME
British twins Lisa and Louise Burns played the Grady Twins in *The Shining* (1980). Film director Stanley Kubrick (1928–99) was inspired by a photograph by Diane Arbus, featuring two identically dressed girls.

PAGE 10
ADVICE FOR MIDWIVES
Page from early modern textbook (1545) by physician Thomas Raynold, who ranks twins as 'difficult births' and recommends special management.

FRONT COVER
TWIN PORTRAIT
Photograph of twins taken from Luigi Gedda's *Twins in History and Science* (1961). Courtesy University of Florida, George A. Smathers Libraries.

BACK COVER
THE DOLLY SISTERS
Hungarian-American identical twins Rosie and Jenny Dolly perform at a burlesque club at the height of their fame in the 1920s. Photo: Heritage Art / Heritage Images via Getty Images.

❋ ❋

First published in the United Kingdom in 2023 by Thames & Hudson Ltd, 181A High Holborn, London WC1V 7QX

Twinkind © 2023 Thames & Hudson Ltd, London

Text © 2023 William Viney

Foreword © 2023 George Viney

For image copyright information see p. 221

Designed by Sara Ozvaldic at Barnbrook

British Library Cataloguing-in-Publication Data

A catalogue record for this book is available from the British Library

ISBN 978-0-500-02626-7

Printed and bound in China by C&C Offset Printing Co. Ltd.

MIX
Paper | Supporting responsible forestry
FSC® C008047

Be the first to know about our new releases, exclusive content and author events by visiting
thamesandhudson.com
thamesandhudsonusa.com
thamesandhudson.com.au

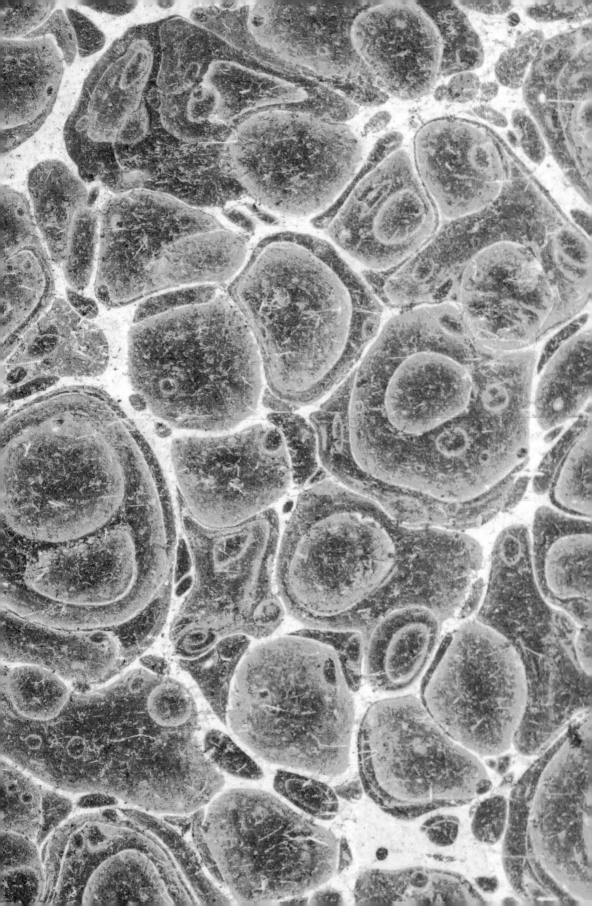

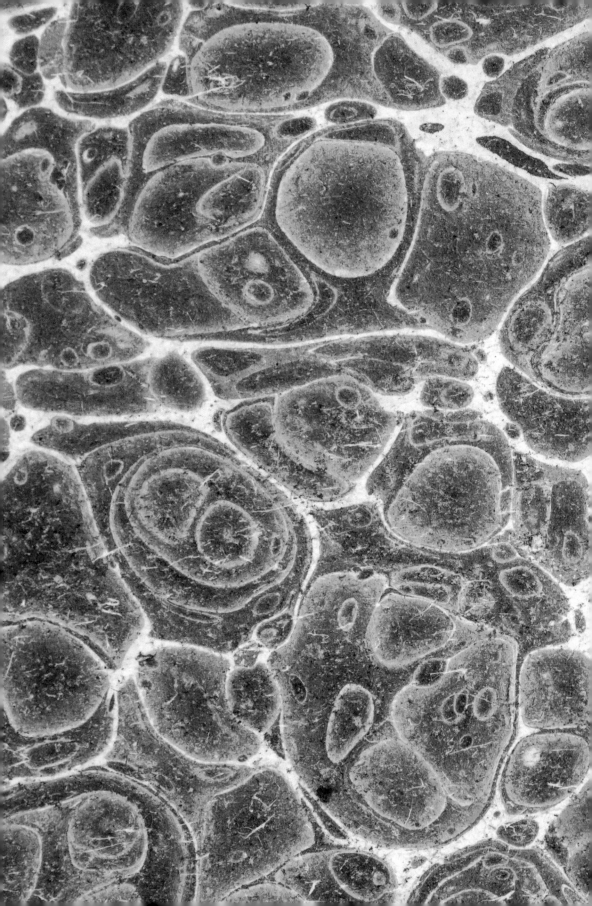